SEEING THE
UNSEEN REALM

Destinies Revealed

You will know them by their fruits.
Do men gather grapes from thorn bushes
or figs from thistles? Even so, every good tree
bears good fruit, but a bad tree bears bad fruit.
(Matthew 7:16-17)

JAMES A. DURHAM

TABLE OF CONTENTS

Acknowledgements

This book came as a gift from the Lord. I want to express my thanks first and foremost to Him for providing the revelation for this book and for inspiration along the way to complete it.

I want to acknowledge the invaluable assistance I received from my extremely blessed, highly favored, and anointed wife, Gloria. I am grateful for her dedicated and tireless assistance in proof reading the text and confirming the accuracy of the scriptural references. I also want to acknowledge my daughter, Michelle, who remains a constant and consistent cheerleader throughout the process of all my writings. In the last several months, Michelle has asked almost daily about my progress on the book. I am so thankful to the Lord that He placed both of these two amazing women in my life and constantly blesses me through their love and support!

INTRODUCTION

Some people limit their experience of spiritual sight by establishing the wrong expectations. The Lord can do things in many different ways. Some people will only be happy if they see angels. Others will only be content if they see visions of the Lord. Many will only accept their gift if they have a Third Heaven visit and see the Lord's Throne Room. I want to suggest something completely different for you. How about asking to see who you truly are in Christ. Ask the Lord to let you see yourself as He sees you. Pray that the Lord will reveal your purpose and destiny in the Kingdom. Think on this as you study the passage below and seek to understand it from Jesus' point of view. He is giving you a model for your own spiritual development.

> *I am telling you now before it happens, so that when*
> *it does happen you will believe that I AM who I AM.*
> (John 13:19, NIV, 2011)

In one of the most recent editions of the New International Version (NIV) of the Bible, the verse as written above represents a significant change in the interpretation of this passage from the original language. When I first read it, I stopped to meditate on the deep meaning in this passage. Most people living in the time when Jesus made this statement did not know who He really was.

They imagined all kinds of things about Him. Even His disciples struggled to fully grasp who He was.

Many people today are still struggling to understand who Yeshua truly is. To make it clear to His disciples and for people today, He gave a prophetic word about the one who would betray Him. Then He told them that when it happened they would understand by revelation knowledge who Yeshua was. The same promise given in that prophetic word is available to you. You can look at the fulfillment of His words and know that He was a genuine prophet of God who was truthful in all He said and did. Remember what He said in John 14:6-7, *"Jesus said to him, 'I am the way, the truth, and the life. No one comes to the Father except through Me. If you had known Me, you would have known My Father also; and from now on you know Him and have seen Him.'"* Yeshua not only spoke the truth. He was and still is the truth.

If it was difficult for people in His day to know who Yeshua was in relationship to the Father, how much more difficult is it for people to know who you truly are in the spiritual realm? Yeshua knew who He was, but others couldn't fully grasp it. One of our great struggles in becoming disciples is to fully grasp not only who He is, but who we are to Him. We cannot know this by worldly wisdom. We cannot get help from advisors who only know how the world looks at us. The good news is that we have not been left without hope or help. I like the way the verse below was translated in The Message Bible.

> *And now I'm going to tell you who you are, really are. You are Peter, a rock. This is the rock on which I will put together my church, a church so expansive with energy that not even the gates of hell will be able to keep it out.* (Matthew 16:18, TMG)

Do you know who you really are? This may seem like an odd question, but I believe it is a very important question. I meet many people who are desperately seeking to find out who they are sup-posed to be. Peter seemed to be one of those persons. He had a great destiny in the Kingdom of God, but he was unaware of that fact. When Jesus gave Peter the prophetic message above, he still didn't fully grasp what it meant. He definitely did not know how high the Lord intended to lift him or how far the Lord planned to take him as an apostle.

This raises another important question. Do you know who the Lord says you are? What did He mean in Matthew 5:13 when He said, *"You are the salt of the earth"*? Perhaps you can share Peter's challenge at this point. What does Jesus mean when He compares you to a rock or to salt? At times you just have to wait in faith and see where the Lord will take you. On the other hand, you have help in understanding it right now. The Holy Spirit has been sent to guide you into all truth. As you study this book, con-tinue to ask the Spirit of truth to guide your understanding.

You have a calling from Father God. You are called to belong to Jesus Christ. You are called for a great purpose in the Kingdom of God and to a great destiny in your service for Him. Most spir-it-filled believers know that, but many still do not know exactly what they are called to do or destined to be. How about you? Do you know precisely what the Lord is calling you to do and to be? Paul was very surprised to find out what the Lord planned for him to be and to do. He was headed in the wrong direction and it took a bolt of lightning to wake him to his destiny. Later he tried to help others understand their calling.

> *Through him and for his name's sake, we received grace and apostleship to call people from among all the Gentiles to the obedience that comes from faith. And you also are among those who are called to belong to Jesus Christ.* (Romans 1:5-6, NIV)

One of the most important declaration made by the Apostle Paul is that all believers belong to Jesus Christ. If you are His, then you must be ready to become all He plans for you to be. Tragically, many people are still struggling with powerful feelings of unworthiness, and seem to be brought low by self-doubt. Low self-esteem can prevent you from being all the Lord is calling you to be. The enemy constantly tries to keep self-defeating thoughts in your mind. You need to take authority over your mind. It is very important for you to begin to believe in your heart and in your mind what the Lord says about you. Read it aloud often and let Him take captive the thoughts that block you from your destiny.

> *Therefore I say to you, do not worry about your life, what you will eat or what you will drink; nor about your body, what you will put on. Is not life more than food and the body more than clothing? Look at the birds of the air, for they neither sow nor reap nor gather into barns; yet your heavenly Father feeds them.* **Are you not of more value than they?** *Which of you by worrying can add one cubit to his stature?* (Matthew 6:25-27)

Often people who are suffering from low self-esteem have difficulty grasping what Jesus said in the passage above. Through this decree, He is telling you that you have great worth. You have great value to the Father, to the Son and to the Holy Spirit. Don't let the enemy steal your self-confidence or your knowledge of who you are in the Kingdom. You are a creation of the Lord. He didn't make a mistake when He made you. He didn't make a mistake when He called you. Be aware that He can see beyond what you see. He understands things in your future which are not visible to you right now. Consider another powerful teaching of Jesus:

> *So why do you worry about clothing? Consider the lilies of the field, how they grow: they neither toil*

*nor spin; and yet I say to you that even Solomon
in all his glory was not arrayed like one of these.
Now if God so clothes the grass of the field, which
today is, and tomorrow is thrown into the oven,
will He not much more clothe you, O you of little
faith?* (Matthew 6:28-30)

How can we doubt God's promises of provision for us?
The problem is we have been trained in the educational system
of the world. With worldly wisdom, you cannot understand
the spiritual things of the Kingdom. No corporate body in this
world would have chosen the twelve men the Lord made apostles. They didn't meet the basic criteria for employment in the
world, but they were perfect in all their imperfections for the
purposes of the Lord. The first step in seeking understanding is
to stop evaluating yourself by the standards of the world. You
are not in a popularity contest and you are not likely running for
some great office in government. You are called to do the work
of the Lord, and you are perfectly suited for His purposes. Stop
worrying about all the things others are saying and let the Lord
do His supernatural work in you and through you.

*Therefore do not worry, saying, "What shall we
eat?" or "What shall we drink?" or "What shall
we wear?" For after all these things the Gentiles
seek. For your heavenly Father knows that you
need all these things. But seek first the kingdom of
God and His righteousness, and all these things
shall be added to you.* (Matthew 6:31-33)

Now, is the time to seek the kingdom of God and His righteousness! Father God decreed that in Christ Jesus you are righteous. He gave this to you as a free gift from the finished work
of Yeshua ha Messiach. Now, He wants to give you more and
more, but you need to be ready to receive these gifts from the

Lord. Now is the time to cast off all restraints imposed by those who are not being led by the Spirit of the Lord. Now is the time to believe everything He said about you.

> *Jesus answered them, "Is it not written in your law, 'I said, "You are gods"'? If He called them gods, to whom the word of God came (and the Scripture cannot be broken), do you say of Him whom the Father sanctified and sent into the world, 'You are blaspheming,' because I said, 'I am the Son of God'? If I do not do the works of My Father, do not believe Me; but if I do, though you do not believe Me, believe the works, that you may know and believe that the Father is in Me, and I in Him.* (John 10:34-38)

This is a very difficult thing for most people to grasp. How can we even begin to believe something like this? You have to begin by confessing that you believe everything that Jesus taught. Then confess that what He says about you is true and His words are completely trustworthy. Remember what He said in John 14:12, *"Most assuredly, I say to you, he who believes in Me, the works that I do he will do also; and greater works than these he will do, because I go to My Father."* I advise people to read this aloud over and over until it becomes anchored in their hearts and minds. Remember what Paul wrote in Romans 10:17, *"So then faith comes by hearing, and hearing by the word of God."* Read it aloud right now so that you can hear the word of God being spoken into your heart.

Now read aloud Psalm 82:6, *"You are gods, and all of you are children of the Most High."* Do you believe it now? If not, continue to read these powerful destiny releasing words aloud until they become real to you. You must always remember that you were created in His image. Like Him, you are a speaking spirit who releases power through your words; especially when they are also His words. Now look at the passage below and see if the Lord is speaking to you about who you are in Christ. Don't focus on what your mind is saying. Focus on what the Holy Spirit is saying about you.

> *Now you are the body of Christ, and each one of you is a part of it. And in the church God has appointed first of all apostles, second prophets, third teachers, then workers of miracles, also those having gifts of healing, those able to help others, those with gifts of administration, and those speaking in different kinds of tongues. Are all apostles? Are all prophets? Are all teachers? Do all work miracles? Do all have gifts of healing? Do all speak in tongues? Do all interpret? But eagerly desire the greater gifts.* (1 Corinthians 12:27-31, NIV)

The Lord has given us many ways to confirm His word in our lives. We need to apply all of these if we are going to fully understand His Word. First, look at what the Lord says and does. Then look at what you are saying and doing. Like Jesus you should be saying what you hear Him saying and doing what you see Him doing. As you begin to live and minister this way, fruit is produced in your life and work. Think about the teaching below and do some very honest soul searching about your own walk with Him. Do people see spiritual fruit being produced through you? Do they see the Lord working with you and through you or do they see you doing your own thing?

> *For every tree is known by its own fruit. For men do not gather figs from thorns, nor do they gather grapes from a bramble bush. A good man out of the good treasure of his heart brings forth good; and an evil man out of the evil treasure of his*

> *heart brings forth evil. For out of the abundance*
> *of the heart his mouth speaks.* (Luke 6:44-45)

What kind of fruit is being manifest in and through your life? If it is not what you want it to be, please do not get into self-judgment and condemnation. That is what the enemy does. Satan is the accuser. Don't do his work. Instead, turn to the Holy Spirit and ask His help to guide you into a lifestyle of bearing spiritual fruit pleasing to the Lord. The purpose of this book is to help you do this very thing. As you study the book, ask yourself all the questions you see and be honest with yourself and the Lord. Then ask the Holy Spirit to work in and through you to produce the kind of good fruit Jesus taught us to bear.

Many people see you for what you are not. They focus on your past mistakes, failures and missed opportunities. For these people, whatever you do in the present will be measured by your so-called shortcomings. This attitude on the part of others attempts to box you in and prevent you from rising higher than your past. People like this will always focus on your limitations and ignore your potential. They can tell you more about what they believe you cannot do than they can articulate who you are or who you can be in Christ. Do not let their words prevail. Do not accept their limitations.

Some people see you for what you are right now. This seems liberating if you have lived under the oppressive spirit of the first type of person. Upon closer observation this is not much better than the first type, because it tends to box you in where you are. Rather than seeing your potential, these people try to pressure you to become content with who and what you are right now. They may not think it is much, but it is better than nothing. They may even try to discourage you from trying to improve your circumstances. As with the first group, do not let their words prevail.

The Lord has a very different way of looking at you. He created you and He knows the potential He placed in you from the moment of your conception in His mind. He sees you for what He has destined you to be. He sees far beyond your past or you present and He wants to help you rise to your highest level of anointing. This is why He often sends prophetic words which point to a potential outcome rather than your current circumstances. He alone knows who you are from the very beginning and it is His plan to lift you higher and higher into the very image of who you were created to be. Listen to what He is saying to you in the passage below.

> *Now the Lord is the Spirit; and where the Spirit of the Lord is, there is liberty. But we all, with unveiled face, beholding as in a mirror the glory of the Lord, are being transformed into the same image from glory to glory, just as by the Spirit of the Lord.* (2 Corinthians 3:17-18)

Now is the time to listen to the Lord. This is the season to hear what He is calling you to be and what He is anointing you to do. He sees you for who you really are in spirit, soul, and body. You are who He created you to be. You are who He gifted you to be. You are anointed to bear much fruit for the Kingdom of God. The purpose of this book is to help you see it and to become who you really are in Jesus Christ. Should you choose to accept it, this is your challenge. I am believing in you and praying that you will succeed in amazing and wonderful ways.

> *If the world hates you, keep in mind that it hated me first. If you belonged to the world, it would love you as its own. As it is, you do not belong to the world, but I have chosen you out of the world. That is why the world hates you.* (John 15:18-19)

If you are not of the world, where are you from? You are a citizen of the Kingdom of God and you have been sent into this world as an ambassador of King Jesus and Father God. Paul says it this way in Ephesians 2:19, *"Now, therefore, you are no longer strangers and foreigners, but fellow citizens with the saints and members of the household of God,"* One way to know who you are is to get a firm grasp on your citizenship. You are a citizen of Heaven sent to earth with a purpose. Who are you? *"You are the light of the world. A city that is set on a hill cannot be hidden."* (Matthew 5:14) You are who the Lord says you are. You are who He created you to be and it is time for you to know what that means. Amen?

PRAYER

Father God, open the eyes of my heart. Open my spiritual eyes to see what you are showing me in this season. Open my spiritual ears to hear what you are speaking to me right now. Cover me with the robe of humility so that I can handle the truth from your perspective. Let me continue to be in awe of who you are. Give me a heart of wisdom so that I can have the proper "fear of the Lord." Give me the spiritual tools to accomplish your purpose in my life. Show me my true destiny so that I can begin the journey you have set before me. Here am I Lord. Send me! I pray that all I do and say from this moment forward will bring you glory, honor and majesty. I pray these things in humility. I pray these things in the mighty name of Yeshua ha Messiach. Amen and Amen.

PART ONE

LIFTING THE VEIL OF DECEPTION

Today was another classroom day in Heaven. We still have much to learn in order to be ready as the bride for the return of Yeshua our Bridegroom. Between the resurrection and the ascension, the Lord gave the disciples an advanced course in the principles of the Kingdom of God (Acts 1:3, "*After his suffering, he showed himself to these men and gave many convincing proofs that he was alive. He appeared to them over a period of forty days and spoke about the kingdom of God.*") We need this advanced course in these last days in order to take our stand for the truth of the Gospel of the Kingdom. We must be open to learn more about the Kingdom of God than we have ever known before! Much of the Lord's teaching was given to reinforce things He had already taught. The Lord is also releasing a fresh understanding and urgency to these teachings because the time is at hand.

This heavenly visit was not a very pleasant experience in the beginning. The Lord began by showing us some of the false teachings already present in the church. These manmade doctrines are rapidly growing in intensity. The Lord said, "A time of growing levels of deception has now begun and is about to increase dramatically! You must be prepared for it." Then the Lord showed us in graphic form some of the works the enemy is about to release.

In this vision, I saw the woman John described in Revelation 17:3-5, "*So he carried me away in the Spirit into the wilderness. And I saw a woman sitting on a scarlet beast which was full of names of blasphemy, having seven heads and ten horns. The woman was arrayed in purple and scarlet, and adorned with gold and precious stones and pearls, having in her hand a golden cup full of abominations and the filthiness of her fornication.*" She revealed herself to the people and many chose to follow her in the ways of the flesh and abandoned the Lord. This was a very unpleasant thing to see, and it spoke of the time at hand when there will be a great falling away in the church. We know this will happen, but I still pray that more people will be saved from it.

Then the Lord let us see people claiming to have prophetic words from Him, but the things they were saying were contrary to the Word of God. Many people received these words and gave up the teachings of the Lord. In addition, there were many false teachers who were leading people to accept current social and political teachings be released by socialist organizations and the governments of this world. People were being drawn into popular but flawed notions of political correctness and inclusiveness. The actions of these people clearly reveal how contradictory their teachings are. At the same time they are claiming to be totally inclusive of all beliefs and various religious groups, they are condemning the Word of the Lord and rejecting those who followed Him. We were shown people who claimed to be believers who were making a preferential choice to be socially acceptable while rejecting their calling to stand strong for the Lord. This is the wrong choice in these days of increasing darkness. We could clearly see in the heavenly classroom that their poor choices were taking them further into the kingdom of darkness and further from the kingdom of light.

At this point, I was reminded of a teaching of Jesus recorded in Mark 13:21-23, *"Then if anyone says to you, 'Look, here is the Christ!' or, 'Look, He is there!' do not believe it. For false christs and false prophets will rise and show signs and wonders to deceive, if possible, even the elect. But take heed; see, I have told you all things beforehand."* (See also Matthew 24:23-25) For me this was a very sad and painful thing to accept. I began to ponder some important questions. Will some of us actually be deceived to the point of following the false teachings and deceptions of the world? Are some of us moving toward the kingdom of darkness? Are some being deceived and led away from the Kingdom of Light?

The Lord's teaching was very clear. If we do not stay in the Word of God and remain close to the Lord, we are at great risk right now. We need to pray earnestly for greater gifts of discerning of spirits. May we discern the work of the Holy Spirit and follow Him! May we discern the work of the enemy and reject him and all his false teachings! May we stand strong in the Lord! Remember and hold to James 4:7, *"Therefore submit to God. Resist the devil and he will flee from you."* This is so simple and yet so powerful!

I pray that we will walk in the promise of James 4:8, *"Draw near to God and He will draw near to you. Cleanse your hands, you sinners; and purify your hearts, you double-minded."* Lord Jesus come quickly and cleanse our hands and purify our hearts that we might be delivered from this deception. Draw us continuously into your presence, power, wisdom, and light! Amen and Amen!!!! This was the end of the vision.

FALSE PROPHETS AND FALSE TEACHERS

> *But there were also false prophets among the*
> *people, even as there will be false teachers among*
> *you, who will secretly bring in destructive her-*
> *esies, even denying the Lord who bought them,*
> *and bring on themselves swift destruction. And*
> *many will follow their destructive ways, because*
> *of whom the way of truth will be blasphemed. By*
> *covetousness they will exploit you with deceptive*
> *words; for a long time their judgment has not*
> *been idle, and their destruction does not slumber.*
> (2 Peter 2:1-3)

As you consider the reality of false prophets and false teachers, it is important to understand the Lord's revelation in John 10:10, *"The thief does not come except to steal, and to kill, and to destroy. I have come that they may have life, and that they may have it more abundantly."* The enemy has always used false teachers and false prophets to work out his evil and destructive plan in your life. In order to be all you were created to be, you need to be set free from all the oppressive spirits which attempt to discourage you and make you see yourselves as less than you truly are in Christ. The enemy wants to impart a spirit of judgment and condemnation on you. All false teaching is designed to put a veil over your eyes. The goal of all such teaching is to prevent you from seeing what the Lord plans for you. It is time to be set free from everything which hinders you.

The Lord has a completely different and far better plan for your life. Read His promise again: *"I have come that they may have life, and that they may have it more abundantly."* The Lord wants to release abundance into your life. He wants to release the Spirit of life (Romans 8:2) to give you victory and to bring His abundance to you. To accept these gifts you must let go of all manmade traditions and false teachings. This is not an easy challenge, but it is necessary if you are going to reach the fullness of your destiny in the Lord. Many well-meaning teachers are releasing things which are false. They teach what they have received. They are also deceived. In the remainder of this book it is my intention for you to be released from all these false teachings and from every veil of deception. It is time for all these harmful things to be lifted off of you. Amen?

Chapter One

RELEASING THE SEER ANOINTING

During an outpouring of the Lord's Glory in a church meeting, I was given an amazing and humbling vision. In the vision, I was kneeling before the Lord in a different way than I had ever experienced before. My left knee was on the ground while my right foot was firmly planted on the floor. This position looked something like the way movies portray knights bowing before their king. My head was bowed low in humility and awe before the Lord. I was wearing my robe of humility. This robe is very old and well worn. It seems to have been brown at one time, but is now faded with age.

As I bowed before the Lord, he moved to my left side and said, "Would you like to see how I see you?" With my head still bowed low, I said that I would like to see this. In this vision, I was outside myself and watching this from a position slightly behind and to the right of where the Lord was now standing. He had a staff in His right hand and used it to slowly pull back my old tattered robe. Underneath the robe, I began to see something like a knight in shining armor. The armor was made of gold and seemed to almost be on fire as the light of His glory reflected from it.

As the Lord pulled the robe back from my head and left shoulder, I was overcome with the fear of the Lord and wanted to be certain that I did not let a spirit of pride into my heart. I asked the Lord to put the robe back over my head. He covered me as I had asked. I felt so very unworthy of what I saw and realized that I am much more comfortable with the robe of humility. I have been very reluctant to share this experience with others, because it could easily be taken the wrong way. This experience did not result in a spirit of pride. It was an extremely humbling experience as I sensed deeply my unworthiness for what the Lord was showing me.

As I began writing this book, I became more and more convinced that I must share what the Lord revealed to me. I know now this vision was not for me alone. It was also for you. As the Lord encouraged me to share this experience, I became convinced that I should have allowed the Lord to show me all He wanted me to see. He honored my request to stop seeing these things. I now know this was a mistake on my part. In this season, the Lord wants us to see who we really are in the Kingdom of God. We need to deal with our issues of pride vs. humility so He can give us the revelation we need. This kind of revelation is released to give us a clear picture of who we should be striving to become for the Kingdom of God in order to give glory to the Father, the Son and the Holy Spirit. The first challenge is to get our focus off of ourselves and squarely back on Him.

In most cases, the Lord's view of who we are created to be is much higher than our self-image. He sees the destiny and purpose for which He created us. He sees how we will look when we faithfully complete our mission for the Kingdom. I was reminded of what Paul wrote in 2 Timothy 4:8, *"Finally, there is laid up for me the crown of righteousness, which the Lord, the righteous Judge, will give to me on that Day, and not to me only but also to all who have loved His appearing."* Are you ready to see what the Lord has in store for you? Are you ready to truly see who you are in Christ?

I believe that this is the season for spirit-filled believers to have their spiritual eyes opened to see who they have been called to be. Remember: when these things are revealed, you will not be filled with pride. You will be filled with humility when you see how far you need to go to reach this position. You will be infinitely aware (as I was) that this is not about your righteousness or goodness. This is about what the Lord has done for you on the cross. In His grace, He has chosen to bestow these things on you. It is important for you to understand fully how you are to use these gifts from the Lord in the future.

> *Whenever the living creatures give glory and honor and thanks to Him who sits on the throne, who lives forever and ever, the twenty-four elders fall down before Him who sits on the throne and worship Him who lives forever and ever, and cast their crowns before the throne, saying: "You are worthy, O Lord, to receive glory and honor and power; for You created all things, and by Your will they exist and were created."* (Revelation 4:9-11)

Seeing and understanding these things requires the use of the wisdom of the Lord. We have not been left without resources. The wisdom of the Lord is available to us here and now. Remember James 1:5, *"If any of you lacks wisdom, let him ask of God, who gives to all liberally and without reproach, and it will be given to him."* This is an awesome promise from the Lord. Remember how He gave wisdom to Solomon when He asked. He will do the same for you when you ask. As you seek the wisdom of the Lord, remember that even with this great wisdom, Solomon struggled to understand the deep things of the Lord.

> *He has made everything beautiful in its time. He has also set eternity in the hearts of men; yet they*

*cannot fathom what God has done from begin-
ning to end.* (Ecclesiastes 3:11)

As you reflect on the words of Solomon in the passage above,
remember that he wrote these things on the other side of the
cross. He went through all his soul searching and struggles
using only the wisdom of the world. This is a powerful reminder
that worldly wisdom is not sufficient to understand the things
of the Spirit. The Lord granted Solomon great wisdom, but it
only took him a limited distance in his search for the truth. I
believe the Lord wanted Solomon to seek the wisdom of the
Lord when he arrived at these conclusions. Unfortunately he
had deviated from the path of the Lord during the season leading
up to His writing of Ecclesiastes. Without the wisdom of the
Lord, you will never be able to understand God's plan from
beginning to end.

I have some good news. This is not the end of the story. You
and I are looking at these things from this side of the cross and
after the outpouring of the Holy Spirit on all flesh. The gift of
prophesy has been released on all believers through the outpouring of the Holy Spirit. Through the wisdom of the Lord,
you can understand more fully your past, your present and your
future in the Kingdom of God. Before His crucifixion, Jesus
gave a powerful promise to all believers. It is recorded in the
Gospel of John.

> *I still have many things to say to you, but you
> cannot bear them now. However, when He, the
> Spirit of truth, has come, He will guide you into all
> truth; for He will not speak on His own authority,
> but whatever He hears He will speak; and He
> will tell you things to come. He will glorify Me,
> for He will take of what is Mine and declare it to
> you.* (John 16:12-14)

Would you like to know "things to come" in the spiritual realm? Do you want to see into the invisible realm? Since you are reading this book, I will assume that you do. Almost daily, I get requests to impart the seer anointing or to pray for people to have their spiritual eyes opened. At times, this causes me to wonder what has happened to the Lord's people. It seems to me that every born-again, spirit-filled believer should be seeing into the invisible realm. This realm was fully opened for each of us on the Day of Pentecost. Remember how Peter summed up what had happened.

> *For these are not drunk, as you suppose, since it is only the third hour of the day. But this is what was spoken by the prophet Joel: 'And it shall come to pass in the last days, says God, that I will pour out of My Spirit on all flesh; your sons and your daughters shall prophesy, your young men shall see visions, your old men shall dream dreams. And on My menservants and on My maidservants I will pour out My Spirit in those days; and they shall prophesy. I will show wonders in heaven above and signs in the earth beneath: blood and fire and vapor of smoke. The sun shall be turned into darkness, and the moon into blood, before the coming of the great and awesome day of the Lord. And it shall come to pass that whoever calls on the name of the Lord shall be saved.'* (Acts 2:15-21)

Everyone, regardless of their social status, gender, or ethnicity is included in this promise, and you are authorized to receive these promised gifts of the Lord. Each of us should be dreaming prophetic dreams and seeing visions of the Lord. These spiritual gifts have been poured out on all flesh – without exception. All you have to do is accept the gift by faith. People try to make this complicated, but it is very simple. The Lord has already done the work. No waiting is really required for people living in our generation. Don't try to turn it into some complex work that you must complete to become worthy of the gift. It is given because Jesus is worthy and He finished the work on the cross. There is a powerful key given to you in the life of the prophet Elisha.

> *And when the servant of the man of God arose early and went out, there was an army, surrounding the city with horses and chariots. And his servant said to him, "Alas, my master! What shall we do?" So he answered, "Do not fear, for those who are with us are more than those who are with them." And Elisha prayed, and said, "Lord, I pray, open his eyes that he may see." Then the Lord opened the eyes of the young man, and he saw. And behold, the mountain was full of horses and chariots of fire all around Elisha. So when the Syrians came down to him, Elisha prayed to the Lord, and said, "Strike this people, I pray, with blindness." And He struck them with blindness according to the word of Elisha.* (2 Kings 6:15-18)

Has someone spoken over your spiritual eyes and brought blindness to you? It is actually very likely that this has happened. Many false teachers are claiming that all these supernatural spiritual occurrences ended with the original apostles. This is obviously false because these things continued to manifest in the second and third generation of believers referenced in the New Testament. If you have received this teaching and you are having difficulty seeing in the Spirit, you can take some very simple steps to remedy this. Break off these word curses and pray as Elisha prayed.

You don't have to cry out over and over. You don't have to beg God to give you what He has already bestowed on you. Just pray, "Lord open my eyes that I may see." If it doesn't manifest right away, what is the missing ingredient? It is faith. Elisha had absolutely no doubt that his prayers would be answered. Remember, if you pray without believing you are double-minded and can expect nothing. Start again with your spiritual gift of faith. Pray it once and then confess that you believe it and receive it. Begin to give thanks for it even before it manifests. Don't give up. Don't quit. Continue to pray and decree until it becomes a reality for you.

Many people experience another kind of challenge getting their spiritual eyes opened. They have set an unrealistic standard for what they will experience. You cannot control what the Lord gives. Don't get trapped by the enemy into judging the Lord for what you think you didn't receive. If you only see a color, shout hallelujah! Then begin to give God praise and glory. Ask the Holy Spirit to help you understand the revelation in the color. Begin to give the Lord thanks that your spiritual eyes are beginning to open. Then ask for your eyes to be opened more so that you can see more.

Celebrate what you have been given by the Lord. Don't think it is too little. Remember Zechariah 4:10, "*For who has despised the day of small things? For these seven rejoice to see the plumb line in the hand of Zerubbabel. They are the eyes of the LORD, which scan to and fro throughout the whole earth.*" Big things often follow small things. The more you use a gift, the stronger it becomes. When you begin to see, let this happen often. Find out what it means and release what the Lord is giving you to minister. He doesn't give the gift for your entertainment. It always has a purpose. Remember what Peter taught.

And so we have the prophetic word confirmed,
which you do well to heed as a light that shines in
a dark place, until the day dawns and the morning

star rises in your hearts; knowing this first, that no prophecy of Scripture is of any private interpretation, for prophecy never came by the will of man, but holy men of God spoke as they were moved by the Holy Spirit. (2 Peter 1:19-21)

I want to share a great and wonderful revelation I received from the Lord recently. When Moses met with the Lord on the Holy Mountain, he received a profound and wonderful revelation from the Lord. The Lord gave him two stone tablets which had been inscribed by the finger of the God. The words were not written with ink or made with raised letters. The words were in the stone. In reality, Moses couldn't see the letters. He saw the stone still remaining around the letters. The letters themselves were actually invisible. The Lord was revealing something on the mountain that no person had ever seen before. Even righteous Abraham, the friend of God, had not seen the invisible things being revealed to Moses.

The Lord was giving an amazing gift to Moses and through him to all the children of Israel. Before Moses could reveal these things, the people committed a great sin. They made a golden calf and began to worship it as their God. When Moses saw this, he threw the tablets of stone to the ground. The stones broke into many fragments. When the broken stones were on the ground, no one could see anything the Lord had written. What happened to the Word of God written into the stone? Nothing happened to the Word of God. The invisible letters simply went back to Him and waited for Him to write them again after the people repented.

From that moment of revelation on the mountain, the Lord has been revealing unseen things to His people. When we are not in a right relationship with Him, they become invisible again. This isn't the end of the story. When we repent, the Lord restores us and once again lets us see into the amazing invisible realm. He reveals wonderful things that no eye has seen before and no ear has heard. If you need some forgiveness and restoration to get your seer anointing working, don't wait. Get it straightened out with the Lord right now. It is the Lord's will for you to see into the unseen realm.

SEEING BEYOND YOUR CIRCUMSTANCES

It is cold in South Carolina this morning (25 degrees F), and I was enjoying the warmth of my Prayer Shawl (Tallit) as I sang along with one of my old favorite praise songs, "Open the Eyes of My Heart, Lord." As usual, I was singing this song with my eyes closed. At one time that seemed very odd. Then I realized that closing my natural eyes actually helped me see more clearly with my spiritual eyes. As I reflected on this, the presence of the Lord was getting stronger and heavier with each verse. Soon I dropped to my knees covered with the Tallit. As I submitted everything to Him I cried out for the eyes of my heart to open more and more so that I can see Him clearly. His presence grew stronger and soon I was face down on the floor. I asked the Holy Spirit for a word from Heaven for His people today.

Then I seemed to be lifted up into a standing position high above the earth. I was shown a very large white, long-stemmed rose. As I watched, the rose began to open and the purity of the white color seemed to be increasing in intensity. Suddenly something like white flames erupted from the rose and the flames seemed to be leaping up into Heaven and into the very presence of the Lord. Then I heard the Lord say, "Purity and Holiness are the keys to access!" I immediately thought of Hebrews 12:14-16, *"Make every effort to live in peace with all men and to be holy; without holiness no one will see the Lord. See to it that no one misses the grace of God and that no bitter root grows up to cause trouble and defile many. See that no one is sexually immoral, or is godless like Esau, who for a single meal sold his inheritance rights as the oldest son."*

As the phrase *"without holiness no one will see the Lord"* kept going through my mind, I started to see people moving into the flames. The Holy Spirit gave me a revelation about the white rose. It is symbolic of the one true and holy bride of Christ. As people moved into the flames, they were immediately lifted up into the presence of the Lord. I wanted to go with them. So, I stepped into the flames and was lifted up, but I didn't stay very long. I was carried in the Spirit back to the position where I could see the white rose. The Lord said, "You haven't fully understood the revelation of the rose!"

I prayed for the Holy Spirit to give me wisdom, revelation, counsel, might, understanding and the fear of the Lord (Isaiah 11:2). In my prayer I almost left off the phrase, "the fear of the Lord." I suddenly understood something more. The key to purity and holiness is in "the fear of the Lord." Many people today do not like this phrase. They want to be pals with God instead of showing Him honor and respect. The Spirit guided my thoughts to Jeremiah 6:16, *"Thus says the Lord: 'Stand in the ways and see, and ask for the old paths, where the good way is, and walk in it; Then you will find rest for your souls.' But they said, 'We will not walk in it.'"* We need to get back to some of the old paths of the Lord! We need to get back to "the fear of the Lord," if we want to live in purity and holiness. My wife. Gloria, likes to say, "He calls me friend and I call Him Lord." If we want to walk with Him, we must understand who He is and esteem Him above all else.

Then the Lord gave me a vision of someone sitting on a rock on the top of a mountain in Israel. At first, I thought it was Jesus, but the Holy Spirit said that it was Abraham. There was something like a Glory Cloud moving powerfully around him. His eyes seemed to be fixed on something in the distant future. Below where he was seated, I could see his wealth. There was a vast herd of livestock, many tents and more family members and servants than I could count. But, Abraham was not looking at what He had. He was looking into the future to see what the Lord had promised. He was not focused on the things of the flesh, but on the things of the Spirit. The Lord said, "Like Abraham, you need to look beyond your circumstances and get your eyes focused on My promises for you. The People of the white rose look beyond what they have and see what has been promised. These are the ones who ascend to be with Me!"

PREPARING TO RECEIVE THE SEER ANOINTING

Are you seeing all the spiritual truths the Lord wants to show you? Should you be operating in a seer anointing? It is perfectly natural for believers to see visions, dream prophetic dreams and hear the Lord speaking to them. The Bible is filled with beautiful examples of the Lord releasing a seer anointing to His people in order to help them accomplish His purposes in their lives. These examples are in virtually every book of the Bible from Genesis through the Revelation of John. To get a clear and succinct picture of this, you need to look again at the powerful prophetic message given through Joel. Read the prophecy aloud for maximum effect. The reason why you need to do this is found in the teaching of Paul in Romans 10:17, "*So then faith comes by hearing, and hearing by the word of God.*" Hearing the Word of God is a powerful source of faith. It is most effective when it comes from your own mouth. Reading the scriptures this way is a powerful key to assist you in releasing your own seer anointing. I will repeat this teaching of Paul often, because it so important for the development of your spiritual gifts.

> *And it shall come to pass afterward that I will pour out My Spirit on all flesh; Your sons and your daughters shall prophesy, your old men shall dream dreams, your young men shall see visions. And also on My menservants and on My maidservants I will pour out My Spirit in those days.*

35

And I will show wonders in the heavens and in the earth: blood and fire and pillars of smoke. The sun shall be turned into darkness, and the moon into blood, before the coming of the great and awesome day of the Lord. And it shall come to pass that whoever calls on the name of the Lord shall be saved. (Joel 2:28-32a)

In my experience, many people say they believe this prophecy from the book of Joel, but only mean that they believe it is in the Bible. They may also believe that it is for a few other people, but they don't really believe it is for them. This is why I often ask people the question: Do you have flesh? Of course people have flesh, but they need to confess it as they set up the spiritual foundation for opening up these spiritual gifts. Now claim this promise for yourself. Say aloud: "I have flesh and the Lord has poured out His Spirit on me. Therefore, I am enabled to prophesy, dream prophetic dreams and see visions sent from the Lord." Say it aloud over and over. Keep saying it until you own it.

The things which proceed from your mouth come from your heart and also go back into your own heart. Remember what Jesus said in Matthew 15:18, "*But those things which proceed out of the mouth come from the heart, and they defile a man.*" As you read this passage, notice that there are actually two dimensions in this teaching of the Lord. First, the things in your heart come out through your mouth. If you are speaking the promises of the Lord, these things are at least beginning to become a part of who you are. The second part is that the things coming from your mouth also affect your heart. Looking on the positive side notice that the things you speak can not only defile you but can also bless you. When you speak the Word of God through your mouth, you release it in your heart. The more you say it, the stronger it becomes rooted in your mind and spirit. Now go a little deeper as you study the passage below.

For you can all prophesy one by one, that all may learn and all may be encouraged. And the spirits of the prophets are subject to the prophets. (1 Corinthians 14:31-32)

Think about this! Did Paul really say that everyone could prophesy? Many people like to quibble this away so that it has no meaning. On the other hand, I see a promise in it which I claim for myself. Say it with me: "I can prophesy." Now go a little further and claim the second promise. Now that you have this prophetic anointing, your spirit becomes subject to you. Claim it now: "My spirit is subject to me." If you can believe this in your heart and confess it with your mouth, you will release spiritual power into your own spirit. Now speak to your spirit: "Spirit wake up my seer anointing. Open my spiritual eyes to see and my spiritual ears to hear the things the Lord is releasing to me. I believe it. I receive it and I will continuously thank the Lord for it until it manifests fully. Then I will continue to thank Him for this wonderful gift. If you are still having a little difficulty with this, focus on the passage below. Even if you are not currently seer challenged, you will increase your anointing by continuing to claim it.

LOOSING THE SCALES

So Ananias went and found the house, placed his hands on blind Saul, and said, "Brother Saul, the Master sent me, the same Jesus you saw on your way here. He sent me so you could see again and be filled with the Holy Spirit." No sooner were the words out of his mouth than something like scales fell from Saul's eyes—he could see again! He got to his feet, was baptized, and sat down with them to a hearty meal. (Acts 9:17-19)

To jump start his faith and empower his ministry, the Lord gave Paul a physical manifestation of what had been done for him spiritually. The Lord had so powerfully impacted Paul on the road to Damascus that it blinded him. When Ananias laid hands on him, "*something like scales fell from Saul's eyes.*" This was the outward physical manifestation given to confirm that the Lord had opened his spiritual eyes. Paul was wise and had a very good education in the religious beliefs of his people, but he was blind to many of the spiritual realities behind these teachings. The Lord changed all of this, and Paul became a new creation with a powerful destiny and purpose in the Kingdom of God.

Perhaps you would like to have the same manifestation to convince you of the Lord's anointing. Would you like to see scales fall from your eyes? The truth is that you do not need it. There are several reasons why this is true and I want to give you two of them. First, the Lord doesn't keep doing the same things over and over. Remember how He said, "*Then He who sat on the throne said, "Behold, I make all things new.*" Be open to the idea that the Lord may do a completely new thing in your spirit, and it will be the best thing which ever happens to you. Amen? Don't try to be a copy of someone else. The Lord is calling you to be a unique gift to the body of Christ. We are not all the same. We are all unique and important parts of the body of Christ and that is a good thing.

The second reason why you don't need to have scales fall from your eyes is that you can claim what Paul received without actually going through the process yourself. Every promise in the Bible is for you. You just need to claim them. Speak to your spirit right now: "Spirit remove all the spiritual scales I have spoken over my own eyes. Remove all the spiritual scales spoken over me by well-intentioned but incorrect spiritual leaders in the past." Now accept by faith that your spiritual eyes are free to see everything the Lord wants to show you. Claim again your ability to dream prophetic dreams, see visions given by the Lord and hear His voice speaking to you. Remember what Jesus said in John 10:27, *"My sheep hear My voice, and I know them, and they follow Me."* Now speak out the promise: "I am one of Jesus' sheep, therefore I can hear Him speaking to me." Now go a little deeper in the section below.

WHEN HEAVEN OPENS

After these things I looked, and behold, a door standing open in heaven. And the first voice which I heard was like a trumpet speaking with me, saying, "Come up here, and I will show you things which must take place after this." Immediately I was in the Spirit; and behold, a throne set in heaven, and One sat on the throne. And He who sat there was like a jasper and a sardius stone in appearance; and there was a rainbow around the throne, in appearance like an emerald. Around the throne were twenty-four thrones, and on the thrones I saw twenty-four elders sitting, clothed in white robes; and they had crowns of gold on their heads. And from the throne proceeded lightnings, thunderings, and voices. Seven lamps of fire were burning before the throne, which are the seven Spirits of God. (Revelation 4:1-5)

One of the reasons this passage is so powerful is that it clearly states that your circumstances do not limit what the Lord can release to you or through you. Many people who hear these promises start answering with words like, "Yes, but my circumstances make this impossible." Wrong! When John wrote down this powerful revelation from the Lord, he was in exile on the Island of Patmos. He was for all practical purposes on an island prison. His terrible circumstances did not in any way limit what the Lord released through him. Two thousand years later we are still reading and being blessed by what John wrote.

If the Lord could and would do that for John, think about all the things he can do for you and through you regardless of your circumstances. Try to eliminate all the things you speak which begin with "Yes, but..."

Stop making excuses and let the Lord move through you. In addition, stop putting time limits on the work of the Lord. People do this all the time. I constantly hear from people who are impatient because things didn't happen right away. Think about this: the Lord doesn't work on your time schedule. You need to start working on His time table. Amen? Recently several people told me they were worn out waiting for their seer anointing to manifest. Then they told me how long they have waited. I have actually prayed and waited for the gifts longer than some of them have been alive. Don't give up. Don't quit. Keep claiming the gifts by faith.

The enemy wants to use all these circumstances to bring doubt into your heart. Don't let him do that. The enemy doesn't want you to succeed. He has a three-fold plan for you. He will do whatever he can to steal, kill and destroy your destiny in the Kingdom of God. Believe what the Lord has said. Wait patiently for it to manifest. Claim your spiritual gifts before they manifest and begin to pour out words of thanksgiving and praise to the Lord for His awesome blessings. Gratitude will get you a lot further than grumbling. Remember that the things which come out of your mouth can defile you. Make sure that the things you are confessing are in accordance with God's Word. Praise more and complain less. Release thanksgiving for all the wonderful gifts you have received. Try to spend more time and energy giving thanks than complaining about what you have not yet received. Amen?

YOU SHALL SEE THE SPIRITUAL REALM

Therefore, from now on, we regard no one according to the flesh. Even though we have

> *known Christ according to the flesh, yet now we*
> *know Him thus no longer. Therefore, if anyone is*
> *in Christ, he is a new creation; old things have*
> *passed away; behold, all things have become*
> *new.* (2 Corinthians 5:16-17)

This is another multi-dimensional teaching. Many people read this and think about how they should be judging other people or circumstances. People prone to this approach tend to see every kind of admonishment in terms of what it means for other people. In this study, we are looking at the other dimension. What does it mean for you? Another recommendation is that you stop judging what Christ is doing in your life by the standards of the world. Stop evaluating yourself according to the flesh. You are a new creation. Your old limitations, mistakes and failures have passed away. Give them a good burial and move on. Begin to claim and decree that "*all things have become new.*" Now anchor it by decreeing that all things have become new for you. When you are born again into a relationship with Jesus Christ, you will never be the same again.

Taking it a step further, ask a new question based on what your new creation is meant to be. Do you see what the Lord sees in you? The Lord has some key information that He is willing to share with you. He knows exactly what He created you to be. He knows the fullness of your potential. He knows how high you can go in your anointing and how far you can go in the fulfillment of your destiny. Now that your spiritual ears are opened, let Him speak these things into being in your life and work. I also like to claim what the Lord released to Nathanael in the passage below. This promise is for me and it is for you. Amen?

> *Nathanael answered and said to Him, "Rabbi, You*
> *are the Son of God! You are the King of Israel!"*
> *Jesus answered and said to him, "Because I said*
> *to you, 'I saw you under the fig tree,' do you*

*believe? You will see greater things than these."
And He said to him, "Most assuredly, I say to
you, hereafter you shall see heaven open, and the
angels of God ascending and descending upon
the Son of Man."* (John 1:49-51)

Over and over I have claimed these promises for myself.
Now it is your turn to claim them and begin to move in the
power of the Lord's spoken words. Speak aloud: "I will see
greater things." Say it over and over until you believe it. The
nice thing about receiving this teaching in a book is that you
can stop and work on it until it manifests before you move on
to the next part. I encourage you to do that right now. There is
no hurry. It is all in God's timing. You don't have to rush to get
the anointing.

After this promise is anchored in your spirit, move to the
next promise given to Nathanael and claim it for yourself. Speak
it aloud until it is anchored in your mind and spirit. Say aloud,
"I shall see." If you only casually read these things and move
on without taking action, very little is likely to happen for you.
Release the spiritual authority and power the Lord has given to
you by making all these confessions and decrees. Say it again
and again: "I shall see." I remind you that everything in these
promises has to do with the spiritual realm. The Lord opened
Nathanael's eyes to see into the unseen realm. Do you think
Nathanael ever saw these things promised by the Lord? The
Bible doesn't tell us, but I believe the words of Jesus. If He said
it, it happened. Amen?

Now for the next promise. You will see an open heaven.
How cool is that? Think about this for your own spiritual development. Are you ready for it? If you are ready, begin to speak
it into being: "I shall see heaven open." Here is a funny reality.
As I mentioned earlier, I often see better with my spiritual eyes
when my natural eyes are closed. It can work either way, but try
it with your eyes closed. Speak the impartation of Jesus again.

Now let go of any tendency to try to control what the Lord will give you. Let the Lord reveal the things of Heaven which He wants you to see. Don't rush Him. Just wait on the Lord.

Now begin to claim and decree the remainder of Jesus' promise. Do you want to see angels ascending and descending? This is the place to start. This anointing was available all the way back to the book of Genesis. Jacob went to sleep with a rock for a pillow (tough circumstances) and saw heaven open. Study the passage below and see that Nathanael was receiving something originally given to Jacob. If the Lord could do that for them, He can do that for you. Seeing something given twice by the Lord makes it fixed and certain. Just as Nathanael received what had been given in the Word of God to someone else, so can you.

> *And behold, the* LORD *stood above it and said: "I am the* LORD *God of Abraham your father and the God of Isaac; the land on which you lie I will give to you and your descendants. Also your descendants shall be as the dust of the earth; you shall spread abroad to the west and the east, to the north and the south; and in you and in your seed all the families of the earth shall be blessed.* (Genesis 28:13-14)

Did you receive it? If not keep working on it, because there is more. Jesus told Nathanael that he would also see the Son of Man. Obviously he could see Him with his natural eyes at that moment. I believe the Lord was releasing a prophetic promise which would be fulfilled after His ascension. That would be the time when Nathanael and the other disciples would need it most. Think about it. You are living in a time which is also post ascension. Now is your time to see into the spiritual realm. Now is the time to see an open heaven, see angels and see your risen Lord and Savior, Yeshua ha Messiach.

Nathaniel had first been impressed that Jesus knew who he was in the depth of his spirit. Upon first meeting Nathanael, Jesus released a prophetic word which let him know that the Lord knew his spiritual condition completely. *"Jesus saw Nathanael coming toward Him, and said of him, "Behold, an Israelite indeed, in whom is no deceit!" Nathanael said to Him, "How do You know me?"* (John 1:47-48) The Lord also knows who you are in the depth of your heart. He knows if you have or do not have deceit in your heart. He knows everything about you and still gave His life as a ransom for your soul. Now He wants you to know and understand who you are. This is one of the powerful reasons that He is releasing a seer anointing to you.

You are not limited by your past. You are not just someone defined by your personal history of mistakes and failures. You are who and what the Lord created you to be. You need to get free from the past and embrace your future. You need to claim your destiny and accomplish your purpose. This is what the Lord wants for you. This is why He is willing to impart a seer anointing to you. The question remains: Are you willing to accept it and begin to move under the leadership of the Holy Spirit? If you are, then press in for more.

YOU CAN SEE WHO YOU ARE

Arise, shine; for your light has come! And the glory of the LORD is risen upon you. For behold, the darkness shall cover the earth, and deep darkness the people; but the LORD will arise over you, and His glory will be seen upon you. The Gentiles shall come to your light, and kings to the brightness of your rising. "Lift up your eyes all around, and see: they all gather together, they come to you; your sons shall come from afar, and your daughters shall be nursed at your side. Then you shall see and become radiant, and your heart

> *shall swell with joy; because the abundance of*
> *the sea shall be turned to you, the wealth of the*
> *Gentiles shall come to you.* (Isaiah 60:1-5)

I love this revelation which came through the prophet Isaiah, and I am believing that you do too. Otherwise you would not be likely to read this book. You know that this was spoken over God's chosen people. Rest assured that you have been grafted into the root of that promise as well. Look at Romans 11:19, *"You will say then, 'Branches were broken off that I might be grafted in.'"* Did you get that first part? *"You will say."* An important question now is: Will you actually say that? If the answer is yes then say it aloud. *"Branches were broken off that I might be grafted in."* Now say, "I have been grafted in." These promises are for you. Claim them now and hold on to them always.

Take it up another notch by saying, "I have been grafted in to all the promises given to God's chosen people." Now go back to the passage from Isaiah 60, and claim it for yourself: "My light has come and the glory of the Lord has risen upon me." Wow! That felt good when I said it. How about you? Did you really say it and believe it? Think about the depth of that promise. No matter how dark it may get, the light of the Lord's glory is shining on you. No matter how deep and pervasive the darkness may seem right now, you have hope. The lord will soon release something powerful for you. I like to claim another promise from Psalm 30:5, *"For His anger is but for a moment, His favor is for life; Weeping may endure for a night, but joy comes in the morning."* It is always morning somewhere, so accept the gift of His light, His glory and His joy right now.

Now go back to the prophecy given through Isaiah. Read aloud this powerful promise: *"Lift up your eyes all around, and see: they all gather together, they come to you;"* Notice that it first says that the Gentiles will come to you. In essence this means all the nations of the world. This is your anointing to

45

take the Gospel of the Kingdom to the nations. Better still, they will come to you. If you believe it, begin to prepare for it. Let the Lord increase the anointing on you day by day so that when it manifests you are ready. Don't rush it. Let it happen in the Lord's timing. Amen?

The Lord also says that your sons and daughters will return to your love and care. Many families around the world are broken and fragmented today. That is not the Lord's will for you. Do you have estranged family members? Then begin to claim this promise. Speak it aloud over and over. Believe it and receive it even before it manifests. When you truly believe it, you will begin to give thanks to the Lord even before they return. When your heart breaks over the losses in your life, the Lord's heart is hurting more. He wants you to be set free, made whole, and restored in your family relationships. Let this work of the Lord begin in you now by confessing it as if it has already happened.

Think about it: "You shall see." This is confirmed in Isaiah and by Jesus. Claim it from both promise. Right now go back to the promise revealed in Isaiah, Chapter Sixty. *"Then you shall see and become radiant, and your heart shall swell with joy;"* This is such an awesome promise. You will see and it will change you forever. You may start to look like Moses as he came down the mountain with his face glowing with the glory of the Lord which had attached to him. Say it with me: "I shall become radiant." Have you ever noticed that people who really have a deep relationship with the Lord seem to be glowing? Now get ready for it: *"your heart shall swell with joy;"*

Are you willing to walk in this anointing? The remainder of this book is meant to help you move into an anointing to carry all these spiritual gifts. I encourage you again to actually do all the suggested exercises. Speak what you are invited to speak. Believe it, claim it and begin to tell the Lord how grateful you are for what He is doing in your life and ministry. For many people this is an undeveloped side of both their minds and spirits. They have not looked at the seer anointing as a means to see who they truly are in Jesus Christ. It is time to move into the fullness of this blessing. Who are you in Christ? You are who He created you to be and you are who He says you are. Amen?

PRAYER

I am praying for you as I write these things. I am praying:

May the Lord bless you and keep you; May the Lord make His face shine upon you, and be gracious to you; May the Lord lift up His countenance upon you, and establish for you His Shalom. May the Lord put His name on you and bless you now and forever. (Paraphrased from Numbers 6:24-27) May all scales fall from your spiritual eyes so that you can fully embrace the promises of the Lord which are given to release His seer anointing to you! May you see who you are in Christ as He lifts you up from glory to glory into the image of your creation! May you truly become all He created you to be! May you daily experience a spiritual elevation! May the Lord break off everything which hinders you and release you to become a grateful and willing servant of Yeshua ha Messiach in whose name I pray! Amen and Amen!!

Now put this prayer into the first person and pray it over yourself. I recommend that you pray it aloud. I recommend that you pray it often. Let you faith be increased by hearing the Word of the Lord spoken through your own mouth. Expect to increase daily in your seer anointing. Expect to see heaven open. Expect to see angels ascending and descending. Expect to see the Lord and to hear His voice! Expect Him to reveal to you who you truly are in the Kingdom of God. Let it be to you as you have believed. Amen and Amen.

Chapter Two

BREAKING FREE FROM FALSE TEACHING

This morning the Lord gave me a vision which was very unusual and confusing at first. As I went into His presence, I saw the Lord seated on a beautiful and very ornate throne which was covered in pure gold. The Lord was wearing a very majestic and exceptionally ornate robe with beautiful colors of deep red and gold. This doesn't sound very confusing. However, I saw the Lord and the throne upside down. It was as if gravity held Him and the throne on the ceiling and we were standing of the floor. The throne seemed to be moving closer and closer to where we were standing and I didn't understand any of this.

As the Lord came closer, He opened up a series of visions for me of many of the evil and perverse things happening in our world today. Truthfully, I didn't want to see these things. I was very repulsed by the things I was seeing. I think that Ezekiel must have felt something like this when the Lord showed him the perverse things the leaders had drawn and written on the walls of the Temple. Consider how he described these things in the passage below.

And He said to me, "Go in, and see the wicked abominations which they are doing there." So I went in and saw, and there—every sort of creeping thing, abominable beasts, and all the idols of the house of Israel, portrayed all around on the walls. And there stood before them seventy men of the elders of the house of Israel, and in their midst stood Jaazaniah the son of Shaphan. Each man had a censer in his hand, and a thick cloud of incense went up. Then He said to me, "Son of man, have you seen what the elders of the house of Israel do in the dark, every man in the room of his idols? For they say, 'The Lord does not see us, the Lord has forsaken the land.'" (Ezekiel 8:9-12)

As the Lord was showing me all of these things, I was praying for wisdom and revelation to understand what all of this meant. Then the Lord gave me understanding of why this message is important today. As we enter this season of the Kingdom Economy, the enemy will try to hinder the movement of the Lord by getting some of our leaders and people to follow the ways of the world. Many are already being drawn toward the ways of the flesh. As Balaam could not curse Israel because the Lord had blessed them, the enemy cannot put us under a curse. However he is trying to do the same thing he did through Balaam. He is trying to lead us into wickedness so that we bring a curse upon ourselves.

From the throne, I heard the Lord declare, "I am not the one who is upside down! The world and those who live by its values are upside down, but they don't know it! They see everything from the perspective of their position instead of from My Word! You cannot get right side up with upside down thinking or actions!" The Holy Spirit led me to Isaiah 5:20-22, "*Woe to those who call evil good, and good evil; who put darkness for light, and light for darkness; who put bitter for sweet, and sweet for bitter! Woe to those who are wise in their own eyes, and prudent in their own sight! Woe to men mighty at drinking wine, Woe to men valiant for mixing intoxicating drink, who justify the wicked for a bribe, and take away justice from the righteous man!"*

We have entered into a season filled with promise. Great opportunities are coming for the advancement of the Kingdom of God. Because the enemy does not want us to receive this, the level of deception is also increasing. Many are in danger of being led astray. Many are being tempted to follow the world economic system rather than the Lord's Kingdom economy. It is very difficult for people to see what is right and true in these times. More than ever, we need to watch for those who call evil good and good evil. We need to be alert and vigilant over our own hearts to make certain that we do not get caught up in these things.

When I first saw these visions, I felt certain that I was upright and the throne was upside down. This is the enemy's greatest deception in this season. I want to be on the side of the Lord and see from His perspective. May He right everything in our minds and hearts so that we don't get the results described in Isaiah 5:24, *"Therefore, as the fire devours the stubble, and the flame consumes the chaff, so their root will be as rottenness, and their blossom will ascend like dust; Because they have rejected the law of the Lord of hosts, and despised the word of the Holy One of Israel."*

I am praying for you and for me the prayer of Paul in Ephesians 1:15-21, *"Therefore I also, after I heard of your faith in the Lord Jesus and your love for all the saints, do not cease to give thanks for you, making mention of you in my prayers: that the God of our Lord Jesus Christ, the Father of glory, may give to you the spirit of wisdom and revelation in the knowledge of Him, the eyes of your understanding being enlightened; that you may know what is the hope of His calling, what are the riches of the glory of His inheritance in the saints, and what is the exceeding greatness of His power toward us who believe, according to the working of His mighty power which He worked in Christ when He raised Him from the dead and seated Him at His right hand in the heavenly places, far above all principality and power and might and dominion, and every name that is named, not only in this age but also in that which is to come."* Amen and Amen!

RECOGNIZING FALSE TEACHINGS

Why begin this journey of discovery with a chapter on false or manmade teachings? In these humanly inspired teachings you will find the doctrines which are bringing deception into the church's understanding of the character of God's greatest creation. When the Lord created human beings, He said *"It is very good."* False teachers declare the opposite of what the Lord said. False teachers declared that people are basically very bad. They use the term human to represent what is imperfect and without excuse. This is totally contrary to the decrees and workmanship of Father God. He doesn't create defective people or evil beings. His work is *"very good."*

Why would people choose to believe and teach these false things? There are many reasons. I will list a few, but you can probably add several others to the list. Some individuals prefer to bring judgment and condemnation on the Lord's people. They seem to believe this allows them to exercise control over the victims of their abuse. Others criticize so they can feel better about themselves. Some just like to excuse their own bad behavior by placing the blame on God.

It is not supposed to be that way with you. The basic rule of thumb which the Lord has given is for us to love one another as Christ loves us. You have been called to bless others and not speak word curses over them. Even when others try to judge, criticize or harm you, it is your calling to love them and bless them. Remember how Paul said it in Romans 12:14, *"Bless those who persecute you; bless and do not curse."* Jesus took this idea even further. Look at how Jesus said it in Luke 6:27-28, *"But I say to you who hear: Love your enemies, do good to those who hate you, bless those who curse you, and pray for those who spitefully use you."* You should be doing the work of your Lord. Therefore, you must not do the work of the accuser.

> *Then I heard a loud voice saying in heaven, "Now salvation, and strength, and the kingdom of our God, and the power of His Christ have come, for the accuser of our brethren, who accused them before our God day and night, has been cast down. And they overcame him by the blood of the Lamb and by the word of their testimony, and they did not love their lives to the death.* (Revelation 12:10-11)

The enemy is the accuser of the saints of the Lord. As I read the passage above, I began to imagine how tiring that must have been for the Lord to listen to all this judgment, criticism and condemnation day and night, year after year. In the process, the accuser was also blaming God who was their creator. I don't think the Lord wants you or me to pick up where the devil left off. The Lord knows everything about everyone and we don't need to constantly bombard Him with our negative words. Give the Lord a break and bring up your thoughts of praise and thanksgiving for the wonderful people He has placed in your life. He created them and pronounced that His creation was *"very good."* Who are we to disagree with Him?

In addition to accusing the people before the Lord, the accuser has always tried to make believers see themselves as less than they are. You must not listen to Him or get caught up in his accusations against you or other believers. When you participate in making accusations, you are doing the work of the accuser. I don't believe anyone does that intentionally, but the results are the same. I pray for the Spirit of truth to open your eyes and ears to see and hear what the Lord is saying. I pray that He will deliver you from all desire to accuse others. Amen!

I know this is not easy. When I chose to obey the Lord's command to teach about these gifts of the Spirit, Third Heaven visitation and the Open Heaven, I knew that many people would judge and condemn me for this. From the beginning to this very day, the attacks are constant. I have made a fundamental choice. I will bless those who try to persecute me and I will pray for those who want to bring harm to me. When you accept the Lord's anointing, you also accept the responsibility for blessing those who will not receive your ministry. I have found that many of them are unintentionally doing the work of the accuser. Pray for them. They need it. As you know there are people who prefer to do harm to others rather than good. Pray for them anyway.

David declared that evil people are the ones who bring accusations. Psalm 109 (NIV), "*Appoint an evil man to oppose him; let an accuser stand at his right hand.*" It should not to be that way with us. May each of us be set free from any inclinations toward evil! May we never allow ourselves to get caught up in the things the Lord hates! I recommend another careful study of Proverbs 6:16-19 for all those who want to please the Lord. Always remember that the Lord Jesus strictly commanded His followers to refrain from judging and condemning.

> *Judge not, and you shall not be judged. Condemn not, and you shall not be condemned. Forgive, and you will be forgiven. Give, and it will be given to you: good measure, pressed down, shaken together, and running over will be put into your bosom. For with the same measure that you use, it will be measured back to you.* (Luke 6:37-38)

Many people like to quibble about this and diminish what the Lord was saying. What are you actually doing when you take away from the Lord's specific commands and teach man-made doctrines? Be very careful about those who teach this way. This too is false teaching. I have heard many people argue against the teachings of Jesus based on something taken out of context from the Apostle Paul. Paul never intentionally contradicted the words of Jesus or the Word of God. Be careful not to misuse his teachings. Consider what he wrote in 1 Corinthians 4:5, "*Therefore judge nothing before the time, until the Lord come, who both will bring to light the hidden things of darkness, and will make manifest the counsels of the hearts: and then shall every man have praise of God.*" We must defer judging others until the light of the Lord reveals things. Notice that Paul was saying that this time will come after the Lord's return. For now, set aside the work of the accuser.

Why is this so important? To get at the positive messages about your nature, purpose and destiny in the succeeding chapters, you need to break off this deceiving spirit. Without doing this, it will not be possible to fully understand the powerful teachings of the Lord about what He has destined His creation to be and what He has called them to do. Pause a few moments for self-examination. See if you have done or taught any of these things. I believe that all of us have at one time or another fallen short in this area as well as in our walk with the Lord. Most likely we did not do it in order to intentionally disobey the Lord, however the result can be the same for us as well as those we mislead with such teachings. Now is a good time to repent and get a fresh start at teaching all that the Lord commanded with clarity and truth.

> *As I urged you when I went into Macedonia, stay there in Ephesus so that you may command certain men not to teach false doctrines any longer nor to devote themselves to myths and endless genealogies. These promote controversies rather than God's work—which is by faith. The goal of*

this command is love, which comes from a pure
heart and a good conscience and a sincere faith.
Some have wandered away from these and turned
to meaningless talk. They want to be teachers
of the law, but they do not know what they are
talking about or what they so confidently affirm.
(1 Timothy 1:3-7)

The presence of false teachers is a reality in our lives. It has always been this way, however we do not have to be fooled by them. In order to avoid this error, we must be careful about what we hear as well as what we say. Notice Paul's advice to Timothy: *"The goal of this command is love, which comes from a pure heart and a good conscience and a sincere faith."* In addition, think about what Jesus said in Mark 4:24a, *"Then He said to them, 'Take heed what you hear.'"* It is important to understand that you are accountable for what you hear. You choose what you hear and decide what you will listen to in your spirit. Ask yourself whose voice you are listening to in these last days? Are you listening to the voice of the accuser, the voice of worldly wisdom or the voice of the Lord? You don't want to hear the Lord saying to you what He said to the religious leaders who challenged His authority and refused to hear God's truth.

You have let go of the commands of God and are
holding on to the traditions of men. And he said
to them: You have a fine way of setting aside the
commands of God in order to observe your own
traditions! (Mark 7:8-9)

In this brief passage, the Lord mentions twice the error of replacing the commands of the Lord with the traditions and doctrines of man. Do you remember what it means when the Lord says something twice? I believe this teaching is very important to the Lord because He spent so much time teaching it. As in

Jesus' time, most people today do not receive it well when you say this to them. Perhaps the better use of these words of our Lord is to apply them to ourselves. I recommend serious introspection and soul searching in this matter. Paul warned Timothy about a challenging time which was soon to manifest.

> *For the time will come when they will not endure*
> *sound doctrine, but according to their own desires,*
> *because they have itching ears, they will heap up*
> *for themselves teachers; and they will turn their*
> *ears away from the truth, and be turned aside to*
> *fables. But you be watchful in all things, endure*
> *afflictions, do the work of an evangelist, fulfill*
> *your ministry.* (2 Timothy 4:3-5)

I believe that we are living in the time Paul referenced in the passage above. This is the time and now is the season when people are open to many teachings which are not based on "sound doctrine." Many people today have "itching ears," and are chasing after teachers who will tell them what they want to hear rather than the truth of the Lord. We are living in these last days. This is a time when many people have turned *"their ears away from the truth,"* and have *"turned aside to fables."* Don't let false teaching deceive you into being one of them.

Instead of doing these things, Paul calls disciples of Jesus to practice a different kind of obedience. If you consider yourself to be a disciple of Jesus Christ, you are being called by the Lord to be an end-time harvester. You are called and anointed to *"do the work of an evangelist."* You are being called in this way so that you can fulfill your purpose and destiny in the Kingdom. As in Paul's instructions to Timothy, you are being called to this work in order to *"fulfill your ministry."* Ask yourself very candidly how you are doing with your primary mission? Perhaps it is time for some repentance and getting focused back on your first love so that the main thing will still be the main thing.

What kind of disciple will you be if you set aside the teachings of Jesus and begin to teach based on the wisdom of the world? What kind of believer stops believing in the core teachings of the one who has called him or her from darkness into the light? You must be a sincere follower of Yeshua ha Messiach. If you truly represent Him, you will say what He says and do what He does. Amen? This is how Jesus ministered. He only said what He heard the Father saying, and only did what He saw the Father doing. He also stated clearly that the Holy Spirit would minister in the same way (see John 16:13). This is the pattern for us to follow. We must not attempt to do this with words only. We must honor Him with our words, actions, lives and ministries. May we never hear the Lord speak the words below to us because we have failed to follow the commands of the Lord!

> *Hypocrites! Well did Isaiah prophesy about you, saying: 'These people draw near to Me with their mouth, and honor Me with their lips, but their heart is far from Me. And in vain they worship Me, teaching as doctrines the commandments of men.'"* (Matthew 15:7-9)

This presence of false teaching persisted in the early church. Tragically, it continues in the church today. I am praying for a time when the church will rise up and become what the Lord called it to be. I am praying for a time when the church gets back to the basics of its calling and once again focuses on teaching all that Yeshua commanded it to do and to be. I am praying for a time when we will be set free from the spirit of rebellion and the spirit of falsehood (Jude 1:11). May we never be counted with those mentioned by Paul in the book of Titus!

> *For there are many insubordinate, both idle talkers and deceivers, especially those of the circumcision, whose mouths must be stopped, who*

subvert whole households, teaching things which
they ought not, for the sake of dishonest gain.
(Titus 1:10-11)

Many people idealize the New Testament church for the
wrong reasons. They speak as if it was perfect in every way,
however it had the same problems we face today. It consisted
of human beings who often professed more of their weaknesses
than the strengths of the Lord and the power of His teachings.
If you look closely, you will see people today who are twisting
the teachings of the Lord "*for the sake of dishonest gain.*" This
should not be so. Yeshua once asked a powerful and challenging
question, "*For what will it profit a man if he gains the whole*
world, and loses his own soul?" (Mark 8:36)

In spite of all these teachings of the Lord and the other New
Testament writers, the problem persists. False doctrine seems
almost inevitable, but it doesn't have to be that way with us. So
much depends on the truth of the Gospel of the Kingdom. When
we begin to deviate from the path established by the Lord, who
knows how far that can go? Those who are led into deception
begin to be enslaved by the deceiving spirits behind it. The Lord
came to set you free. Don't allow yourself to be enslaved again.

You may be asking again, "Why are we spending so much
time on the subject of false teaching?" Sound doctrine teaches
us who and what we should be in Christ. Remember what the
Lord said in John 8:31-32, "*To the Jews who had believed him,*
Jesus said, 'If you hold to my teaching, you are really my dis-
ciples. Then you will know the truth, and the truth will set you
free.'" Lies and false teachings never set you free. You would
do well to study the passage below and apply it to your own life
and ministry. Remember to read it aloud in order to build your
faith and increase your understanding.

But as for you, speak the things which are proper
for sound doctrine: that the older men be sober,

reverent, temperate, sound in faith, in love, in patience; the older women likewise, that they be reverent in behavior, not slanderers, not given to much wine, teachers of good things—that they admonish the young women to love their husbands, to love their children, to be discreet, chaste, homemakers, good, obedient to their own husbands, that the word of God may not be blasphemed. (Titus 2:1-5)

You are never truly liberated by what is false. It may sound good for a moment, but it will certainly let you down in the end. Remember what Paul wrote in Romans 8:15, *"For you did not receive a spirit that makes you a slave again to fear, but you received the Spirit of sonship. And by him we cry, "Abba, Father."* To really know and understand who you are in Christ Jesus, you must be set free from every spirit of bondage. False teachings lead to bondage. This is not the Lord's plan for your life. You are an heir of the Kingdom of God along with Yeshua ha Messiach! Amen? Listen to what Paul wrote in Romans 8:16-17, *"The Spirit himself testifies with our spirit that we are God's children. Now if we are children, then we are heirs—heirs of God and co–heirs with Christ, if indeed we share in his sufferings in order that we may also share in his glory."*

All of these true teachings of the Lord point us toward a powerful understanding of the truth of the Lord. You are not bound by false teachings. You have been set free so that you can be all the Lord created you to be. You can achieve all the Lord destined you to do for the Kingdom. You can have all the spiritual gifts and blessings the Lord has offered to you. You can be elevated by the Lord to operate in these gifts to your maximum potential. You can become more through His truth than by all that the world can teach you about self-actualization and human potential.

You have been called to be a child of the living God and to accomplish amazing and wonderful things all the days of your life on Earth. You are a joint heir with Yeshua ha Messiach. You have been set free from the law of sin and death and elevated to be a part of the Kingdom of the Son of His love. The old has passed away and you are a child of a new and wonderful thing the Lord is doing in your day. The Lord has ordained it and it is wonderful.

> *Therefore, if you died with Christ from the basic principles of the world, why, as though living in the world, do you subject yourselves to regulations—"Do not touch, do not taste, do not handle," which all concern things which perish with the using—according to the commandments and doctrines of men? These things indeed have an appearance of wisdom in self-imposed religion, false humility, and neglect of the body, but are of no value against the indulgence of the flesh.* (Colossians 2:20-23)

Historically, the translators of the Bible have often been afraid of giving the exact meaning of some of the most powerful teachings in God's Word. This is understandable since many of them lost their lives getting the Word of God into the languages of the people. This reluctance is clearly seen in the way they translated Psalm 8. People have believed for many centuries that they were created a little lower than angels. This is simply not an accurate translation of what the Word of God is saying. As you look at Psalm 8, understand that you were created a little lower than Elohim. As you claim the truth of the passage below, begin to believe and receive all this opens up for you.

> *When I consider Your heavens, the work of Your fingers, the moon and the stars, which You have*

ordained, what is man that You are mindful of him, and the son of man that You visit him? For You have made him a little lower than the angels (Elohim), and You have crowned him with glory and honor. You have made him to have dominion over the works of Your hands; You have put all things under his feet, (Psalm 8:3-6)

Some people want to quibble about this passage, and teach that this was only for the Messiah, but that isn't what it says. Even if it did mean that, we would need to interpret it based on what Jesus said in John 14:12, "*Most assuredly, I say to you, he who believes in Me, the works that I do he will do also; and greater works than these he will do, because I go to My Father.*" I am inviting you to stop quibbling away the powerful things the Lord is saying about you. Embrace the truth from His word! As you study the remaining chapters of this book, claim everything the Lord is giving to you. Live by the standards clearly established by Jesus in His powerful teachings; especially in chapters fourteen through seventeen of the Gospel according to John.

PRAYERS

Therefore I also, after I heard of your faith in the Lord Jesus and your love for all the saints, do not cease to give thanks for you, making mention of you in my prayers: that the God of our Lord Jesus Christ, the Father of glory, may give to you the spirit of wisdom and revelation in the knowledge of Him, the eyes of your understanding being enlightened; that you may know what is the hope of His calling, what are the riches of the glory of His inheritance in the saints, and what is the exceeding greatness of His power toward us who believe, according to the working of His mighty power which He worked in Christ when He raised Him from the dead and seated Him at His right hand in the heavenly places, far above all principality and power and might and dominion, and every name that is named, not only in this age but also in that which is to come. (Ephesians 1:15-21)

Show me Your ways, O Lord; teach me Your paths. Lead me in Your truth and teach me, for You are the God of my salvation; on You I wait all the day. (Psalm 25:4-5)

Chapter Three

SEEING AND KNOWING GOD'S PLAN

This morning in my study of the Word and in my prayer time, I kept hearing the Lord speak the words He gave in Isaiah 40:1, "'Comfort, yes, comfort My people!' Says your God." I wondered if there was some special reason why we need to hear this today. Then I realized that we need to hear this every day. We live in the world but we are not of the world. We need to keep our eyes open as we live in a world covered with deep darkness and as the level of deception continues to increase and as the veil thickens over the eyes of so many. We need to hear the Lord speak these words to us: "'Comfort, yes, comfort My people!' Says your God."

I felt myself being lifted up into His presence rather slowly this morning. As the Spirit was carrying me into His presence, I looked up and saw many dark and threatening storm clouds covering the sky over us. But, this was not the end of the story. The enemy does not have the last word over the Lord's people. He cannot maintain this deception or continue to release fear over the bride of Christ. Suddenly the Light of Heaven broke through the clouds with majestic power and great glory. The Glory of the Lord began to rain down over His people, and I heard the

Lord proclaim again, "'*Comfort, yes, comfort My people!' Says your God.*"

As I arrived in the place of His presence, I experienced a very deep level of His Shalom. It seemed like I had moved out from a kind of darkness which wanted to envelop me, and into the Glory which had already come over me and existed within me. Can you feel the presence and His shalom? Can you feel the deep peace and rest the Lord wants to give to you? Can you hear Him decree today: "'*Comfort, yes, comfort My people!' Says your God.*" In His presence, I could feel it! As strange as this may sound, I could see it! In this atmosphere of glory, I could receive His comfort that powerfully. In His presence I could experience much more of the Shalom He has for us. Think about it. Heaven is open and the presence of the Lord is with you wherever you may be. You can receive these things right now where you are.

Then the Lord gave me an open vision. I saw the Lord standing with something in His hands. At first it looked like a very large exercise ball. This seemed a little odd since He was not exercising. As I looked more closely, I could see that He was holding it close to His face and keeping His eyes focused on every detail. Then I realized that it was not a ball. It was the Earth, and He was intently watching over His people. He didn't take His eyes off of His bride. It came into my mind that many people might not like this imagery. Some people don't want to think about the Lord watching them so closely. They want to hide some things from Him. They are choosing to slip back into the darkness from time to time to hide from His awareness. Then the Lord said, "Tell them that I am not watching over them to do harm! I am watching over them to do good for them!" My mind went back to the promise I heard over and over this morning: "'*Comfort, yes, comfort My people!' Says your God.*"

As I continued to watch what the Lord was doing, it seemed like I was able to change my view of the Earth as if looking through a telescope. I could zoom in and see people more closely. I saw a woman who was clinging to the hand of Jesus. She had been crying over her circumstances and had come to Jesus for help. As I watched this vision, I heard the Lord say again, "*'Comfort, yes, comfort My people!' Says your God.*" Then the Lord showed me several men and women who were giving Him their sincere and deep worship. Their eyes were totally on Him as His eyes were focused on them. There was a strong and wondrous connection between the Lord and these people. They seemed to be able to rise above their circumstances and just connect with Him. I realized that these are the ones who have heard and received what the Lord was giving out this morning: "*'Comfort, yes, comfort My people!' Says your God.*" They have already been comforted and are now able to enter into His rest on this Shabbat morning and every day, all day.

The Holy Spirit took me back to Isaiah 40 to release a powerful promise to all His people. The Glory of the Lord is being made manifest to you. Open your spiritual eyes to see His Glory and open your spiritual ears to hear what the Lord is saying to you. We have this promise because it has been spoken out of the mouth of the Lord. Look again at Isaiah 40:3-5, "*The voice of one crying in the wilderness: 'Prepare the way of the Lord; Make straight in the desert a highway for our God. Every valley shall be exalted and every mountain and hill brought low; The crooked places shall be made straight And the rough places smooth; The glory of the Lord shall be revealed, And all flesh shall see it together; For the mouth of the Lord has spoken.'*"

THE LORD HAS A PLAN FOR YOUR LIFE

For I know the plans I have for you," declares the Lord, "plans to prosper you and not to harm you, plans to give you hope and a future. Then you will call upon me and come and pray to me, and I will listen to you. You will seek me and find me when you seek me with all your heart." (Jeremiah 29:11-13, NIV)

During more than forty five years of ministry, the number one question people asked of me was, "What is God's plan for my life?" A closely related question is, "What is God's will for my life?" It seems that a very large number of believers are struggling with these concerns. Perhaps you have asked one or both of these questions in the past. At some point, this is something most people who decide to follow Jesus Christ want to understand more fully. Ask yourself the following questions: How well do I know God's plan for my life? How clear am I about the specific details of His will for me?

If the questions above have concerned you, I have some good news. More accurately, God's Word has some exciting news for you. God has a plan for you, and it is amazing and wonderful!   I often ask people to repeat things during our seminars. I recommend this for you right now. Repeat: God has a plan for me! Amen? Now say, He has an amazing and wonderful plan for me! Keep making these professions until they really sink into your spirit and mind. Then they will truly be yours.

The things which have been happening in your life are not just by chance. God has a plan for you and He is moving you toward the fulfillment of your purpose and destiny. You are not just a pawn in the hands of an angry and capricious God. He wants good things to happen in your life. Sometimes things don't seem very good at a particular point in time. When you go through challenging situations it may be because you have gotten outside the Lord's plan. At other times it may be because the enemy is trying to distract you from your goal. It is important to remember that the enemy wants to block what the Lord is doing through you. After all when you are doing the Lord's will, you are helping to destroy the works of the devil. Remember what Jesus' mission was, *"For this purpose the Son of God was manifested, that He might destroy the works of the devil."* (1 John 3:8b) When you became a disciple of Yeshua ha Messiach, you also began to be a part of the Lord's team which is continuously destroying *"the works of the devil."*

Knowing this, you can understand why he wants to deceive you into failing at your mission.

As a believer, you can know with certainty that failure is not God's plan for you. He wants you to succeed in your Kingdom mission. I have often wondered why this is such a mystery to so many believers. After all, it isn't hidden from us. We have two strong witnesses to the Lord's purpose in our lives. God has revealed it to us through Yeshua (His Living Word) and in the Bible (His written Word). We also have the Holy Spirit who was sent to teach these same truths to us. In reality, the Lord has given us three powerful witnesses to His plan and purpose in our lives. In the last sentence of the verse below, notice the description of God's will. It is *"his good, pleasing and perfect will."* The verses below tell you how to get ready to receive this revelation. Repeat the key points out loud over and over.

> *Therefore, I urge you, brothers, in view of God's mercy, to offer your bodies as living sacrifices, holy and pleasing to God—this is your spiritual act of worship. Do not conform any longer to the pattern of this world, but be transformed by the renewing of your mind. Then you will be able to test and approve what God's will is—his good, pleasing and perfect will.* (Romans 12:1-2, NIV)

You can take this to the bank: God wants you to know His plan. Now repeat that aloud: "God wants me to know His plan for my life!" Amen? Then confess: "I am able to test and approve what God's will is for me." He was so determined for you to know His plan that He had it written down for you. Repeat this declaration often to anchor it in your sprit. The Lord watched over each detail of His message as He inspired the writers of the Bible. He did this to insure that you could hear it correctly and completely. He has done all the hard work. All you have to do is pick it up, study it and accept it. It is as simple as that.

As you read the Word of God, put yourself into each story and each passage. One of the things I have come to believe is that every promise in the Bible is for me. They are also for you. Listen to what the Word says! Believe what He says, and then take it into the depth of your spirit and soul! Finally, make a decision to stand on these promises forever! Remember Paul's instructions in Ephesians 6:13, *"Therefore take up the whole armor of God, that you may be able to withstand in the evil day, and having done all, to stand."* No matter what comes, keep standing on the promises of the Lord and the teachings of His Word. Take Paul's advice in Ephesians 5:17, *"Therefore do not be unwise, but understand what the will of the Lord is."* It is wise to confess what the Lord says. The more you confess it, the better you understand it and the more fully you accept it.

The Lord is very creative in the ways He reveals His plan to us. This is one of the reasons He bestows the seer anointing on all flesh (Joel 2). In visions and dreams, He reveals the plan to those who are open to the Holy Spirit. Joseph had a mission to protect the child, Yeshua, but he didn't really know how to do that. The Lord began to reveal it to him in dreams. Angels came to him and gave instructions in those prophetic dreams. Joseph was always immediately obedient to what he was told in these dreams. The Lord has always used visual images to help people understand His plan. Moses saw the pattern for the Tabernacle and heard the Lord's instructions. With the words and the visions, he knew exactly what to do. Perhaps the Lord is revealing His plan and purpose for you in your dreams or in visions. Like Joseph and Moses, you must immediately obey if you want the Lord to continue to communicate with you this way. This is why we began this study by releasing the seer anointing.

Remember Gods plan and His will are not hidden. God revealed these truths over and over in His Word, through teachings of Jesus, by means of the Holy Spirit and through your own dreams and visions. It is very important to watch carefully what you say. If you continue to speak about what you don't know and what you can't see, you are empowering these negative things to continue and to possibly get stronger. Carefully consider these Biblical truths and begin to confess the outcomes you desire in your relationship with the Lord. Confess that His plan is revealed to you and that you are enabled to see it, hear it, read it and understand it fully in the depth of your heart. Amen?

As you do the things mentioned above, remember that the Lord's will never leads you to a place outside His care and provision. You will never be led to a place where He does not protect you and watch over you. Take the advice given by the Lord in Joshua 1:9, *"Have I not commanded you? Be strong and courageous. Do not be terrified; do not be discouraged, for the Lord your God will be with you wherever you go."* I claim this promise for me and for the ministry. How about you? Speak it aloud to yourself right now. Speak it often. Speak it so often that it becomes stored in your heart like a mighty sword. When you do this, you will become ready and equipped for spiritual warfare. I am aware that I am giving these instructions over and over. I am doing this because it is the way I learned by experience to stand on faith and release these things in my own spirit.

I. GOD HAS A PLAN TO PROSPER YOU

I recommend the following process to you. Read aloud the promise given in Jerimiah 29:11-13. Read it often. Remember the power released when you read God's Word aloud. Another thing to repeat often is Romans 10:17, *"So then faith comes by hearing, and hearing by the word of God."* God's word never comes back void. It always accomplishes His purposes. When you read God's words aloud, you release the same spiritual power Paul was imparting to the believers in Rome. You release the power of God's words to accomplish everything in His will. Think about it! When you read aloud what He wills for you, it releases His power and authority to manifest in your life.

For I know the plans I have for you," declares the LORD, "plans to prosper you and not to harm you, plans to give you hope and a future. Then you will call upon me and come and pray to me, and I will listen to you. You will seek me and find me when you seek me with all your heart. (Jeremiah 29:11-13, NIV)

Now here is a mystery. For some reason, people struggle with this promise. I don't know if they are doubting God's Word or if they are doubting their worthiness to receive it. Always remember that it is not about you or your worthiness. It is about Jesus and what He accomplished for you in His life, death and resurrection. Always keep this in mind when the enemy tries to tempt you to doubt these promises are for you. Jesus paid a great price to make these promises available to you. Do your best to give Him what He paid for on that awful cross. Remember the word of the Lord given in the vision at the beginning of this chapter: "*'Comfort, yes, comfort My people!' Says your God.*"

Many people adamantly reject the ideas of prosperity and blessing. I prefer to echo the prayer from 3 John 1:2, "*Beloved, I pray that you may prosper in all things and be in health, just as your soul prospers.*" I believe the Lord wants to prosper you just as He said through the prophet Jeremiah. This promise is repeated at least 48 times in various places in Scripture. I often wonder if some people simply prefer poverty and suffering. Think about this: Paul said the blessings given to the gentiles are "*to provoke them (Jewish people) to jealousy* (Romans 11:11b)." I can assure you that no Jewish person is jealous of poverty, sickness or brokenness.

Another tragic reality is that many people think God is out to get them. They see Him as some kind of cosmic judge who is waiting for an opportunity to smite them. Many of these people are letting some past failure or mistake haunt them constantly. Well I want to declare to you that you can forget about all your past sins and failures which you have confessed to the Lord! He has chosen to forget them all. Listen to His words in Hebrews 8:12, *"For I will forgive their wickedness and will remember their sins no more."* Think about it! After you make a sincere confession, He has chosen to forget your past. Say it aloud: He has chosen to forget my past! Maybe you need to say it several times until it is anchored in your heart.

Consider this: it is an insult to the Lord when you doubt that He has forgiven and forgotten your confessed sins. When you do this, you are saying that Jesus' sacrifice wasn't enough for you. Listen again to what He says and then believe it. "Then he adds: *"Their sins and lawless acts I will remember no more."* (Hebrews 10:17) Don't take away what He has added for your benefit. You know this promise is fixed and certain because He said it over and over in His Word. It is time to believe that the promises of the Lord are for you. Then receive them and give Him thanks for this indescribably great gift. When you do this you bring Him glory.

Here is the truth according to His Word: God doesn't want to harm you! He is not looking for an opportunity to smite you. He wants to redeem you. He wants to bless you. He wants to prosper you. These are such wonderful promises. Who wants to refuse these gift from His grace? Think about the mistake many people make in this area, and the impact it has on their future. If you don't accept God's plan, the alternative is the enemy's plan for you. Jesus explained this very well in John 10:10a, *"The thief does not come except to steal, and to kill, and to destroy."* That is not the Lord's plan for you. His plan for you is expressed in John 10:10b, *"I have come that they may have life, and that they may have it more abundantly."* I don't know about you, but I prefer Jesus' plan for my life.

As you consider these things, begin to speak aloud some Biblical truths. Say: He does not want to harm me. He has a plan for my life. He plans to bless me! Amen? The enemy has a very different plan for you. Many of the parts of this plan begin with the English letter "D." Consider the list below and personally reject the enemy's plans for you expressed in these words.

DOUBT–To tempt you to question God's word and His goodness

DISCOURAGEMENT – So you will look at your problems rather than God's grace.

DIVERSION – Makes the wrong things seem attractive so you'll want them more than you desire the things of God.

DEFEAT–To get you to see yourself as a failure and stop trying.

DELAY–To make you put off something so it never gets done.

DISEASE – To steal the strength you need to accomplish your purpose.

Don't buy into the enemy's plan for you. He wants to harm you and steal from you. On the other hand, take a step to accept God's plan for your life. Believe it. Accept it. Live it. Then give the Lord thanks for all the good things he is doing in you and through you. The Lord wants to provide for you in every way. Think about His Kingdom math. He prefers to multiply rather than just add to you. Remember the teaching in Hebrews 6:13-14, *"For when God made a promise to Abraham, because He could swear by no one greater, He swore by Himself, saying, "Surely blessing I will bless you, and multiplying I will multiply you."* As a believer, you have received the same blessing. Examine how Paul taught this in the passage below.

Now may He who supplies seed to the sower, and bread for food, supply and multiply the seed you have sown and increase the fruits of your righteousness, while you are enriched in everything for all liberality, which causes thanksgiving through us to God. For the administration of this service not only supplies the needs of the saints, but also is abounding through many thanksgivings to God, while, through the proof of this ministry, they glorify God for the obedience of your confession to the gospel of Christ, and for your liberal sharing with them and all men, and by their prayer for you, who long for you because of the exceeding grace of God in you. Thanks be to God for His indescribable gift! (2 Corinthians 9:10-15)

It is God's plan to prosper you in spirit, soul, and body. Think of it in that divine order of things; spirit, soul, body. Receive every aspect of the promises in the prayer in 3 John 1:2, "*Beloved, I pray that you may prosper in all things and be in health, just as your soul prospers.*" The prosperity of the Lord is not as simple and mundane as mere money. He wants so much more for you. Truthfully, money is the lowest form of Biblical prosperity. The Lord's prosperity comes first to the spirit. Is your spirit prospering in the Lord right now? If not, what are you going to do about it? Begin to believe and receive it. Then confess it and give thanks for it even before it manifests. The Lord's prosperity is based on faith. Remember we don't go by what we see. "*For we walk by faith, not by sight.*" (2 Corinthians 5:7)

Next, prosperity manifests in the soul. The Lord promotes strong mental abilities and gives us a sound mind. "*For God has not given us a spirit of fear, but of power and of love and of a sound mind.*" (2 Timothy 1:7) Without a sound mind and emotional stability we cannot fully appropriate all the Lord has for us. Without a sound mind we cannot live in the fullness of the blessing. The Lord knows this. So one of His wonderful gifts is a sound mind. Confess this promise from 2 Timothy 1:7 over and over until it becomes yours and is powerful in your mind and spirit. Once again remember the word of the Lord given in the vision at the beginning of this chapter: "*'Comfort, yes, comfort My people!' Says your God.*"

The Third aspect of God given prosperity is health. We need strong healthy bodies to do the work of the Lord. This is why so much of the Lord's ministry on earth had to do with healing. This is why He gave gifts of healings to his disciples when He sent them out to do ministry. This is why the Holy Spirit still imparts the gifts of healings today. The Lord cares about your health and is the true source of all healing. In fact, healing is a part of His nature. It is one of His strongest attributes. Think about what He said in Exodus, Chapter fifteen.

> *There He made a statute and an ordinance for them, and there He tested them, and said, "If you diligently heed the voice of the* Lord *your God and do what is right in His sight, give ear to His commandments and keep all His statutes, I will put none of the diseases on you which I have brought on the Egyptians. For I am the* Lord *who heals you."* (Exodus 15:25b-26)

After all these things, you reach the lowest form of prosperity: financial. Even though it is the lowest form of prosperity, it is still a powerful part of what the Lord wants to do for you. He doesn't have a plan to make you suffer in poverty. The enemy sends the spirit of poverty and too many people have embraced it. It is time to be set free and be rid of this oppressive spirit once and for all. Financial prosperity was a part of the blessing given to righteous Abraham. As a believer, you inherit this same blessing.

> *Christ has redeemed us from the curse of the law, having become a curse for us (for it is written, "Cursed is everyone who hangs on a tree"), that the blessing of Abraham might come upon the Gentiles in Christ Jesus, that we might receive the promise of the Spirit through faith.*
> (Galatians 3:13-14)

The main purpose of this promise is for you to *"receive the promise of the Spirit through faith."* It also includes all the other aspects of Abraham's blessing. Father God gave Him great wealth so that he could accomplish the Lord's purposes in his life. This is still the reason for financial prosperity. Deuteronomy 8:18, *"And you shall remember the Lord your God, for it is He who gives you power to get wealth, that He may establish His covenant which He swore to your fathers, as it is this day."* Think about what this means. Through financial prosperity the Lord is establishing His covenant with you. Believe it. Receive it and give thanks until it manifests in your life.

God wants you to share his prosperity plan with others. Too many people who claim to be evangelists go around telling people they're going to hell. Instead of trying to scare them out of Hell, you need to love them into the Kingdom as Jesus did. You are called to let people know that God has a prosperity plan for them, and they don't have to die to get it. This is your inheritance and it is their inheritance from the Lord. You don't die to get an inheritance. Someone else dies to give you an inheritance. Jesus died so that you might be a rightful heir of the blessing of Abraham. Believe it. Receive it. Begin now to confess it and to give the Lord thanks for all He has done for you through the finished work of Christ.

> *But this I say: He who sows sparingly will also reap sparingly, and he who sows bountifully will also reap bountifully. So let each one give as he*

*purposes in his heart, not grudgingly or of neces-
sity; for God loves a cheerful giver. And God is
able to make all grace abound toward you, that
you, always having all sufficiency in all things,
may have an abundance for every good work. As
it is written: "He has dispersed abroad, He has
given to the poor; His righteousness endures forever." (2 Corinthians 9:6-9)*

The Lord's plan for you will never place your eternal soul
in jeopardy. The Spirit of the Lord will lead you to people and
places where He can work through you, lead you, teach you and
guide you. His plan is to give you peace, provision, protection,
prosperity, productivity, power and prophetic words to guide
you. You can trust Him. He has your best interests at heart. He
wants to mold you into the best person and disciple you can possibly be. Believe it. Receive it. Now, begin to give Him thanks
and praise for all He is doing in your life and ministry.

II. GOD HAS A PLAN TO GIVE YOU HOPE

I am going to say it again. Remember to speak all these
promises aloud over and over until you own them. This is how
you activate the promises in your life and ministry. Right now
make a confession of the Lord's plan for you. Speak your destiny into action. Remember the word of the Lord given in the
vision at the beginning of this chapter: "'*Comfort, yes, comfort
My people!' Says your God*." Now say aloud, "God has a plan
to give me hope!" Amen? Speak these powerful decrees over
and over until they manifest for you.

*Blessed be the God and Father of our Lord Jesus
Christ, who according to His abundant mercy has
begotten us again to a living hope through the
resurrection of Jesus Christ from the dead, to an*

*inheritance incorruptible and undefiled and that
does not fade away, reserved in heaven for you,
who are kept by the power of God through faith
for salvation ready to be revealed in the last time.*
(1 Peter 1:3-5)

It is a tragic reality that many people live in hopelessness today. It is as if hopelessness has become an epidemic and spreads like a virus throughout the populations of our world. Many people have just given up. All of their worldly sources of hope have failed. What can you do when all seems lost? The one thing you can always do is return to God. The Lord is your source of hope. In fact, He is your only true source of hope.

Hope is wonderful, but hope alone is not enough. Consider what the writer of Hebrews 11:1 was saying, *"Now faith is the substance of things hoped for, the evidence of things not seen."* For your hopes to be realized you must add faith to the formula. It is faith that produces substance for the things hoped for. How can you build up your faith? Remember the verse we used earlier. Romans 10:17, *"So then faith comes by hearing, and hearing by the word of God."* You were created in God's image. He is a speaking spirit. You are also a speaking spirit and there is power in your words; especially when you say what the Lord says. With faith, you go beyond what you can currently see. You can receive the unseen promises and wait in faith-filled patience for them to manifest. Confess what Paul wrote in Romans 8:25, *"But if we hope for what we do not see, we eagerly wait for it with perseverance."* This is powerful. When you hope for the unseen realities you also receive the gift of perseverance. Faith brings power to increase your trust that the Lord will keep all His promises which He has given to you. Now believe this: God wants to reveal his love and purpose for you.

*Therefore, prepare your minds for action; be
self-controlled; set your hope fully on the grace*

to be given you when Jesus Christ is revealed.
As obedient children, do not conform to the evil
desires you had when you lived in ignorance. But
just as he who called you is holy, so be holy in all
you do; for it is written: "Be holy, because I am
holy." (1 Peter 1:13-16, NIV)

This is real hope. This is Biblical hope. It is based on and strengthened by faith. Consider what Paul really means in Romans 8:24, *"For we were saved in this hope, but hope that is seen is not hope; for why does one still hope for what he sees?"* Paul is speaking about saving hope. You don't hope for what you already possess. There is no need for hope after you receive it. It is prior to the manifestation that you need to stand on the power of hope.

I urge you again to believe that every promise in the Word of God is for you. Now, hope for it with this kind of hope. Believe it long before you receive it. Be filled with gratitude for all the Lord will do for you in the future. Now that is hope! There is a powerful reason for this, and it is not just about us. Our purpose in the Kingdom is to win others to the Lord. One of the powerful uses of hope is to let it manifest in your confessions. You see, God wants you to tell others about this hope.

Thus God, determining to show more abun-
dantly to the heirs of promise the immutability
of His counsel, confirmed it by an oath, that by
two immutable things, in which it is impossible
for God to lie, we might have strong consolation,
who have fled for refuge to lay hold of the hope set
before us. This hope we have as an anchor of the
soul, both sure and steadfast, and which enters
the Presence behind the veil," (Hebrews 6:17-19)

While you wait for the promises of the Lord to manifest, remember: His plan for you will never take you out of the blessed peace and love which constantly surround and embrace you. His mercies will always sustain you. They never fail and they never run out. You can declare with the prophet, *"Through the Lord's mercies we are not consumed, because His compassions fail not. They are new every morning; great is Your faithfulness."* (Lamentations 3:22-23) The Shalom of God is always with you to protect you from every spirit of fear and to release the authority of the Lord to accompany all you are doing for the Kingdom.

III. GOD HAS A PLAN TO GIVE YOU A FUTURE

Take a moment to decree the words of this section. Say, God has a plan to give me a future! Now repeat it several times until it is anchored in your spirit. David said in Psalm 37:37, *"Mark the blameless man, and observe the upright; for the future of that man is peace."* The Hebrew word David used was "Shalom." This word in its original meaning is much more than peace. When I pray for Shalom, I always express it with seven words: peace, provision, protection, prosperity, productivity, power and prophetic words. When the Lord provides everything you need, you will most certainly experience peace. This is Shalom. Shalom is your future with the Lord. Remember the word of the Lord in the vision at the beginning of this chapter: *"'Comfort, yes, comfort My people!' Says your God."*

The Lord's plan for your life provides the promise of a multidimensional future. There is first a promise of a long term future for you. This is peace with God. This is eternal. It helps you to know and trust that this lifetime is not all there is. The Lord provides for you now and has already made provision for your eternal hopes to be realized. His plan is greater than your hope. The future He promises will be greater than you can imagine. God has an eternal plan for all His family. It is for those who choose to walk with Him during this lifetime.

> *So He said to them, "Assuredly, I say to you, there is no one who has left house or parents or brothers or wife or children, for the sake of the kingdom of God, who shall not receive many times more in this present time, and in the age to come eternal life."* (Luke 18:29-30)

He also has a plan for your short term future. Notice in the passage above that Jesus said you will receive much more "*in this present time.*" This is not just a nebulous promise to be realized in some distant future. The promise is for you to receive benefits here and now. The Lord has a future for you in this present lifetime. Remember, you don't inherit things after you die. That's not an inheritance. You have inherited because Jesus died for you, and that is also for now.

The Lord wants you to begin to grasp an eternal view of these things in the here and now. The peace (Shalom) of God is for now, and it is His plan for you to live in this experience with other believers during this lifetime. However, this is not an early retirement plan. You don't just stop working and expect the Lord to provide. He provides for you through others. In addition, He wants you to provide for others from what He sows into your life. In John 4:36, Jesus said, "*And he who reaps receives wages, and gathers fruit for eternal life, that both he who sows and he who reaps may rejoice together.*" You are to accept these blessings, but you don't just rest in them. What you do with His gifts now will be a determining factor for what you receive in your eternal future. It is all tied together in Yeshua.

One further point is that God wants you to tell others about His plan for their future. Here is an old saying which I think I may have made up: It's not: "Here's the score — just us four and no more." Jesus loves everyone, and God has a future for them. How will they know unless someone tells them the Good News? Who will go for Him? Who will tell them these wonderful promises? Will it be you?

> *How then shall they call on Him in whom they have not believed? And how shall they believe in Him of whom they have not heard? And how shall they hear without a preacher? And how shall they preach unless they are sent? As it is written: "How beautiful are the feet of those who preach the gospel of peace, who bring glad tidings of good things!"* (Romans 10:14-15)

Remember this: The Lord's plan and His will for your life will never leave you lacking in either His Shalom or comfort. He will constantly provide for you in spirit, soul and body. You can trust Him. He promises to go with you and to accompany your work and proclamations with healings, signs, wonders and miracles. His presence will always be with you. You can be assured that you are never alone and without resources. It is time to believe it, receive it, and give thanks for it.

CONFUSED ABOUT GOD'S PLAN?

You don't need to be among those who are in confusion. Begin to make that a reality in your life. One way to do this is to stop speaking and confessing your confusion. Start speaking your faith! Begin to confess the Word of God. Begin to make powerful decrees about His promises and live as if you have them before they manifest. Say to others, "Of course we know God's plan. It is clearly written in The Word of God." It is all in the Bible whether you know its location or not. Trust that He can lead you to it and through it. Remember: The Holy Spirit is speaking it into your spirit.

Say this aloud: God has provided all I need in His Word. Some people say, "But, it's so hard to understand it all!" Don't confess this with them. Confess what God's Word says. The Lord will help you to understand it. Remember: it's spiritually discerned. Remember 1 Corinthians 2:14, *"But the natural man does not receive the things of the Spirit of God, for they are foolishness to him; nor can he know them, because they are spiritually discerned."* If you don't think you have the necessary wisdom to understand, I have some good news: God gives wisdom to those who ask.

> *If any of you lacks wisdom, let him ask of God, who gives to all liberally and without reproach, and it will be given to him. But let him ask in faith, with no doubting, for he who doubts is like a wave of the sea driven and tossed by the wind. For let not that man suppose that he will receive anything from the Lord; he is a double-minded man, unstable in all his ways.* (James 1:5-8)

Get these Biblical truths into your heart and stand on them in faith until they manifest. Continue to read the promises aloud. Don't forget Romans 10:17, *"So then faith comes by hearing, and hearing by the word of God."* Speak it and hear it! Now confess aloud: I will speak it! I will hear it! My faith will increase! Remember that both acts (reading and hearing) store it in your heart. Now confess: I will store it in my heart! One of the powerful keys to putting this into action is to start by getting right with God.

In the little monthly devotional book prepared by the Radio Bible Class, *"Our Daily Bread,"* June 2, 1992, I read about an instant cake mix that was a big flop. The instructions said all you had to do was add water and bake. The company couldn't understand why it didn't sell. Their research department discovered that the buying public felt uneasy about a mix that only required water. Apparently people thought it was too easy. So the company altered the formula and changed the directions to call for adding an egg to the mix in addition to the water. The idea worked and sales jumped dramatically.

Many people have the same reaction to God's plan for their life. It sounds too easy and simple to be true. It is a challenge for many people to believe that salvation is not a reward for the good things they have done. Remember what Paul said in Ephesians 2:8-9, *"For by grace you have been saved through faith, and that not of yourselves; it is the gift of God, not of works, lest anyone should boast."* Unlike the manufacturer of the cake-mix, God has not changed His "formula" to make it more marketable. It may sound too easy, but it's still free. Just ask and it will be given to you.

PRAYER

Father God, I come to You in the Name of Jesus. I thank You for your promise to prosper me; to give me hope and a future. I confess my faith in your Son, Yeshua ha Messiach. I put my trust in His Name. I will worship you and love you forever. Please help me to accept all your promises by faith and to live out the plan you have for me. Give me boldness to share this good news with everyone I know as well as everyone I will meet in the future. I pray this in the mighty name of *Yeshua Ha Messiah*! Amen and Amen!

Have the faith of Job and declare: *"For I know that my Redeemer lives, and He shall stand at last on the earth; and after my skin is destroyed, this I know, that in my flesh I shall see God, Whom I shall see for myself, and my eyes shall behold, and not another. How my heart yearns within me!* (Job 19:25-27, NIV)

PART TWO

DESTINIES REVEALED IN SPIRITUAL FRUIT

As I lifted up praise to the Lord this morning, I began to sense the presence of angels of holiness in our worship room. I welcomed them and sincerely wanted them to minister what the Lord sent them to do. Then the Spirit of Holiness began to manifest and the power of His presence shifted the atmosphere in the room. Remember that Biblical holiness is being set apart for God and then being consecrated for His work and dedicated to His service. At this point Evan Levine's song, *"The Aaronic Blessing,"* began to play, and I cried out to the Lord to put His fire on my head and burn away everything that hindered the flow of His Spirit in me. The fire of the Lord began to burn and I cried out for more fire. As I went face down in worship, the power of His presence covered me and I was carried in the Spirit to many different places in visions of the Lord.

The Holy Spirit told me that He is releasing a powerful anointing on those called to be evangelists and pastors. Some will hear the call for the first time today to step into one of these two offices of ministry. Some will hear it again because they have not yet accepted it. Some who have received it and are waiting for the anointing of the Lord will receive it today. As I received these things, the fire of the Lord continued to intensify in my hands and it is still burning like coals of fire. The Lord desires to set us on fire for the ministry today. As promised in the Word of God, there is a baptism of fire being released. If you desire this baptism, lift up holy hands and let the Lord pour it out on you and into to you. Let it consecrate you for service as it burns away everything which has hindered you in the past. Let it release a new passion to save souls and to train and equip the saints for their service in the Body of Christ.

Then the Lord lifted me up to the training center in Heaven. As I watched a powerful release of the Glory of God began to penetrate into the heads of the people I was watching. The light of His fire and glory began to burn away things in the people who were open to receive it. Do you need this today? It is available to you. This was a message for you! The first thing I saw being burned away was a generational curse which had limited a woman for a long time. The Lord just pulled it out and burned it up in the fire of His Glory. Next, some other family curses were removed and burned. This is a day to be set free and delivered from all those things which have hindered you and blocked the flow of the Holy Spirit in you. Just receive it and let the Lord do the work He wants to do for you today. Finally, all kinds of fleshly things were burned away in many different people, and the power of the Spirit of Holiness was set loose in them. The transformation was awesome for everyone willing to receive it today. I remembered Romans 12:2, *"And do not be conformed to this world, but be transformed by the renewing of your mind, that you may prove what is that good and acceptable and perfect will of God."*

As I write this message, my hands continue to burn with the fire of the Lord and I can still feel the presence of the Spirit of Holiness and the angels of holiness. The work is continuing for all who are willing to receive it. At this point the Holy Spirit led me to Titus 3:4-7, *"But when the kindness and the love of God our Savior toward man appeared, not by works of righteousness which we have done, but according to His mercy He saved us, through the washing of regeneration and renewing of the Holy Spirit, whom He poured out on us abundantly through Jesus Christ our Savior, that having been justified by His grace we should become heirs according to the hope of eternal life."*

To this point, all of this was like receiving really good news. I kept saying all morning, "The Lord is good! And, His mercy endures forever!" Even in the midst of these affirmations, the Lord showed me some who were not willing to receive what He was releasing today. As I watched, they were removed from His presence and from the Body of Christ. I was reminded by the Spirit that in a time of great grace those who reject it are removing themselves from the source of grace, healing, restoration and power. This was an awesome and fearful thought until I realized that it was coming from the Spirit of Grace Who desires to protect all of us from making the wrong choices today or any other time. I pray that you will be open to receive everything the Lord is releasing! I pray that you will allow Him to transform your mind, renew your soul, and set your spirit on fire! Amen and Amen!

KNOWN BY YOUR SPIRITUAL FRUIT

For you were once darkness, but now you are light in the Lord. Walk as children of light (for the fruit of the Spirit is in all goodness, righteousness, and truth), finding out what is acceptable to the Lord. And have no fellowship with the unfruitful works of darkness, but rather expose them. For it is shameful even to speak of those things which are done by them in secret. But all things that are exposed are made manifest by the light, for whatever makes manifest is light. Therefore He says: "Awake, you who sleep, arise from the dead, and Christ will give you light." (Ephesians 5:8-14)

Are you becoming more and more aware of who you are in Christ? Are you seeing more and more in visions and prophetic dreams? Continue to decree that your seer anointing has been activated and you will see the Lord's plan and destiny for you. As you do this, continue to go to the Word of God to learn more of what He says about you. Ask the Holy Spirit to guide you into all truth. The Lord's plan and purpose for you is part of that truth.

Listen to what Paul is saying about you: "*you are light in the Lord*." There may be days when you don't feel like the light of the Lord. Remember, you are not to go by your feelings. You are to live by faith. Claim again that every promise in the Bible is for you. Say it aloud right now: "I am the light of the Lord. I will walk as a child of the light, I will produce the '*fruit of the Spirit*.' I will walk in "*goodness, righteousness, and truth*." It is very important to make these confessions rather than speaking the accusations of the enemy. You are more likely to produce the fruit of the Spirit if these are your confessions.

Each believer needs to make a fundamental choice between being dedicated to a lifestyle which produces the fruit of the Spirit or living in a manner which brings forth the unfruitful works of darkness. If you are reading this book, you have most likely made the right choice. The remainder of Part Two of this book focuses on the kind of fruit the Spirit wants to produce in and through you. It is always my prayer that the Spirit of wisdom and revelation will be with you to give you even more revelation in studying this than I received in writing it. I am also praying that the Spirit of truth will be a constant companion and guide assisting you to live a fruitful life which will be pleasing to the Lord.

In the next three chapters, I will share with you one of my strong beliefs about the fruit of the Spirit. In Galatians 5:16-26, Paul lists nine specific fruits of the Spirit. The prophetic significance of the number nine is "divine perfection." Within this list of nine, I find three groups of three. This also relates to the concept of divine perfection. Three is a powerful number prophetically. It is often understood to relate to how the Lord reveals Himself as Father, Son and Holy Spirit. The Lord created us to be manifest in three unique ways: spirit, soul, and body. The realms of creation are also seen as Heaven, Earth and Hell. In Paul's list of the fruits, three are to bless us, three are to bless others, and three are to bless and honor the Lord.

Chapter Four

VISIBLE BY FRUIT IN YOUR LIFE

Face down before the Lord, I went into an open vision. I was lifted high above a part of the earth which I did not recognize, but I liked it very much. I was positioned with the Lord looking down on a beautiful area where the ocean met this exquisitely beautiful land lined with amazing sandy shores. The area behind the beach front was covered with trees and plants richly adorned in deep shades of green which spoke of fruitfulness and prosperity. My eyes were drawn to a mountain range of solid rock which protruded far out into the ocean. I watched as large and powerful waves hit this extended mountain range. It seemed to be a protective barrier established across the front of the peaceful shore. Then I heard the Lord speak. He said, "I have established a protective shield around you and your nation. Many people are not even aware of it or the fact that I established it for them. They are just going about their business as usual and attributing their prosperity to their own wisdom, worth and work. They do not acknowledge me or express any gratitude for what I have done. You must be aware that I established it and I can take it away."

Then I saw the hand of the Lord come down and grasp the mountain as if He was standing ready to remove the protective shield over our nations. My thoughts immediately went to the news article from Israel which I read this morning. In the article, many sources were saying they had been put on alert that our President and Secretary of State are traveling to Israel and other Middle Eastern nations in an attempt to force Israel to divide the land and establish a Palestinian State within the nation of Israel. My thoughts went to Zechariah 2:8-9, *"For thus says the Lord of hosts: "He sent Me after glory, to the nations which plunder you; for he who touches you touches the apple of His eye. For surely I will shake My hand against them, and they shall become spoil for their servants. Then you will know that the Lord of hosts has sent Me."* Then I thought and prayed, "Oh Lord! Here it comes again! When will they ever learn?" I feel a deep need for all of us to be in intercessory prayer for all the nations in the United Nations which are supporting the dividing of the land of Israel. It is time for the intercessors to build a wall and stand in the gap for their nations. The wrath of God is coming and only His intercessors can stand in the gap now!

I was suddenly and very abruptly lifted out of this experience and carried to Heaven. I found myself standing partially inside the branches of a huge tree looking at the fruit which was growing there. I knew exactly where I was, because I had been there several times before, however, I had never seen any fruit which looked like this. There were leaves on branches all around my head and I made plans to eat the leaves (which bring healing to the nations), but at this point I was more focused on the fruit. The fruit was shaped like an ear of corn, but was not corn. The part which resembled the shape of the kernels of corn looked like impenetrable scales. It looked rough and hard, but I was certain that I was supposed to eat from the fruit this morning. I took the fruit which had been offered and was totally surprised at how easy it was to peel the fruit like a ripe banana. The meat of the fruit was very unusual but tasted delicious. This may be hard to imagine, but it tasted like a fruit salad with bananas and citrus fruit combined. I ate the entire thing and felt so refreshed.

Then I heard the Lord say, "It is very important to eat from the Tree of Life now! Things are coming and you need to be built up and strengthen to be ready for it! When the protective shield is lifted, difficult times are coming, but you must not be anxious or afraid! The fruit of the Tree of Life will be available to you through all the challenging times which are coming. You can come and eat whenever you choose. However, right now you must build up the power of life in your body to be made ready! As you eat the fruit, areas in your spirit need to be opened to receive a more powerful anointing of the presence of the Spirit of Life! This is urgent and extremely important right now!"

I pray that you and I will continuously have access to the Tree of Life, the fruit, and the healing leaves! May we be obedient to the Lord and build ourselves up with His nourishment now so that we will be ready for whatever may come! May we be set free from all anxiety and fear and filled with trust for the Lord and His plans for us! May we all experience a profound calling for effective intercession over our nations! Troubles are coming to many nations and we all need to stand together in agreement as we pray! Remember what Jesus said, *"Most assuredly, I say to you, he who believes in Me, the works that I do he will do also; and greater works than these he will do, because I go to My Father. And whatever you ask in My name, that I will do, that the Father may be glorified in the Son. If you ask anything in My name, I will do it."* (John 14:12-14)

SEEK FRUIT IN YOUR LIFE

I say then: Walk in the Spirit, and you shall not fulfill the lust of the flesh. For the flesh lusts against the Spirit, and the Spirit against the flesh; and these are contrary to one another, so that you do not do the things that you wish. But if you are led by the Spirit, you are not under the law. Now the works of the flesh are evident, which are: adultery, fornication, uncleanness, lewdness, idolatry, sorcery, hatred, contentions, jealousies, outbursts of wrath, selfish ambitions, dissensions, heresies, envy, murders, drunkenness, revelries, and the like; of which I tell you beforehand, just as I also told you in time past, that those who practice such things will not inherit the kingdom of God. But the fruit of the Spirit is love, joy, peace, longsuffering, kindness, goodness, faithfulness, gentleness, self-control. Against such there is no law. And those who are Christ's have crucified the flesh with its passions and desires. If we live in the Spirit, let us also walk in the Spirit. Let us not become conceited, provoking one another, envying one another. (Galatians 5:16-26)

In the previous chapter, I attempted to answer the question: Does God have a plan for your life? Of course the answer is "YES!" The plan does not include any desire of the Lord to harm you! He is the source of good and perfect gifts. It may sound painfully obvious to you, but many people do not seem to know this. Even people who say they are believers often fail to understand this. I do not want this to be true of you any longer. That is why I ask you to repeat things over and over. I do this because I believe it is very important for people to know and believe this truth about the Lord. He has a plan to prosper you and give you hope and a future.

HOW DO YOU KNOW IF YOU ARE IN THE WILL OF GOD?

You will know them by their fruits. Do men gather grapes from thorn bushes or figs from thistles?

Even so, every good tree bears good fruit, but a
bad tree bears bad fruit." (Matthew 7:16-17)

It sometimes amazes me that people can seem so confused about the will of God. After all, there are over 300 references to it in the Bible. I believe that it is time for the body of Christ to quit speaking confusion about the kingdom. We need to stop saying that we don't understand. If we lack understanding, we have resources to help us. We have the Holy Spirit and we have the written Word of God. In His farewell address, the Apostle Paul declared, *"I have not hesitated to proclaim to you the whole will of God."* (Acts 20:27) Paul did all he could to release the entire will of God to the people he taught. It is a part of God's will and His plan for you to receive it and then reveal it to others.

If you have questions about the will of God, don't worry. It is revealed in His written Word. If you have an automated Bible on your computer, phone or tablet, look up some of the references to the will of God. You have a treasure trove of powerful revelation knowledge at your fingertips. You also have Yeshua ha Messiach, the living Word of God. He has a complete and total understanding of the will of God for you, and He wants to share it with you. In the passage below, take note of how Isaiah describes the Messiah.

> *There shall come forth a Rod from the stem of*
> *Jesse, and a Branch shall grow out of his roots.*
> *The Spirit of the Lord shall rest upon Him, the*
> *Spirit of wisdom and understanding, the Spirit of*
> *counsel and might, the Spirit of knowledge and*
> *of the fear of the Lord.* (Isaiah 11:1-2)

It is time to make a fresh start at living in the wisdom of the Holy Spirit. I say again: forget about the past and stop focusing on what didn't happen or what you didn't receive. Now is the time to embrace the promises of the Lord, and to move in the knowledge and understanding He gives. This is the time to get your eyes fixed on what God is doing and what He will soon do for you and through you. In other words, you need to get into the will of God and become who He has called and equipped you to be. Claim all these promises given to you. Confess them aloud so that they will become anchored in your mind and heart. Amen? From this frame of reference, study the passage below and put it into practice in your life and work for the Lord.

> *And do not be conformed to this world, but be transformed by the renewing of your mind, that you may prove what is that good and acceptable and perfect will of God.* (Romans 12:2)

SPEAKING WHAT THE LORD SAYS

It is time for us to intentionally strive to speak what God has said and what He is now saying. Remember that is what Jesus did. After all, He is our example of how to live for the kingdom in a manner which will bring honor and glory to Father God. Consider what Jesus said in John 12:50b (NIV), *"So whatever I say is just what the Father has told me to say."* Remember that this is also exactly what the Holy Spirit is doing, and He is our guide and spiritual coach.

> *But when he, the Spirit of truth, comes, he will guide you into all truth. He will not speak on his own; he will speak only what he hears, and he will tell you what is yet to come.* (John 16:13)

Did you catch the last part of this passage? One of the promises is that the Spirit of truth will tell you *"what is yet to come."* I claim this promise regularly. It is foundational to operating in a seer anointing. You can believe and receive this promise for your life as well as for your destiny. The Holy Spirit will tell you things to come in your life. He will show you what you are to become. He will even guide you to know how you will look when you are fully operating in this anointing.

It is time for you to fully submit to the Father and willingly put the Spirit of God in charge of your life. You need to make a fundamental choice each day whether you will try to run your life or let Him take charge and guide your spirit in accordance with the will of the Father. Are you tired of trying to do your will and failing to see it manifest? Have you done your best, but it doesn't seem to be good enough? Has it sometimes seemed like there is little fruit in your ministry for the Lord? If you have answered yes to any of these questions, I have good news for you. One thing is certain: when the Holy Spirit is in charge, you will produce fruit in abundance. If you want to be fruitful and pleasing to the Lord, put the Holy Spirit in charge of your daily walk.

This is actually one of the main ways you can know if you're in God's will. You are known by your spiritual fruit. Make a sincere and honest evaluation of your own life. What kind of spiritual fruit are you producing? Not only will others know you by the fruit of your life, but this is how the Lord sees and knows you. Is the fruit of your life a blessing to Him, to others and to yourself? Does the fruit in your life bring glory and honor to the Lord? Are others seeing the fruit listed in the following passage of scripture in your life and work?

> *But the fruit of the Spirit is love, joy, peace, long-suffering, kindness, goodness, faithfulness, gentleness, self-control. Against such there is no law.*
> (Galatians 5:22-23)

The passage above names the nine fruits of the Spirit revealed to the Apostle Paul. As I pointed out earlier, there are actually three unique groups of three fruits of the Spirit identified in this list. Prophetically the number three points to completeness.

These fruits of the Spirit will bring fullness and completeness into your life, your ministry, and your relationship with the Lord. Our ways are often flawed, but the Lord's way is always perfect. God's way is so awesome, because everything in our lives and our relationships will be in perfect harmony.

FRUIT FOR YOUR OWN LIFE

In this chapter, we will focus on the first three fruits of the Spirit; love, joy, and peace. I believe that these are the fruits of the Spirit which manifest in your life to bless and enrich your experiences of the Lord's glory. It is also true that others will be blessed when these fruits are manifesting in you and through you, however the main focus is on what this fruit will do for you personally and spiritually. Think about what your life will look like when all of this fruit is flowing forth from your spirit. Activate your seer anointing and let the Lord reveal it to you.

1. LOVE

When you are recognized by your spiritual fruit, you can be certain that you will be recognized by your love. Love is its own reward. Think about it! We live by and in accordance with what we give. The Father is the greatest of all givers and we have been created in His image. His love is so powerful that it is correct to say God is love. Remember what John wrote in 1 John 4:16, "*And we have known and believed the love that God has for us. **God is love**, and he who abides in love abides in God, and God in him.*" Do you believe that you were created in His image? If you believe that you are His creation, then expect to become more and more like Him. This doesn't mean that you will occasionally or often demonstrate some degree of love for others. This means that you are becoming love just as He is love.

Those who live in such a way that love is one of the primary products of their relationship with the Lord are truly lovely people. Do you know someone like this? One of my best early childhood memories is of a time when I was sitting in Miss Smalley's Sunday School Class. She was one of the most loving people I have ever known. Her love had more influence on me than all of the other teachers combined. Love is powerful. It can change the lives of those around you. You can be certain that those who love with the Father's love are also loved by Him in return. Study the passage below and seek to understand fully what the Lord is commanding you to do.

> *A new commandment I give to you, that you love one another; as I have loved you, that you also love one another. By this all will know that you are My disciples, if you have love for one another.* (John 13:34-35)

Love is the mark of a faithful and true disciple of Yeshua ha Messiach. The Lord said, *"If anyone loves Me, he will keep My word; and My Father will love him, and We will come to him and make Our home with him."* (John 14:23) This is the litmus test of true discipleship. Without love you cannot bear the fruit of the Kingdom. Without love you cannot be truly obedient to the Lord. Without love He will not abide with you.

Love is also a powerful witness to the world. When people see the love we have for one another, they will know that we follow Jesus. Love is your constant witness to everyone you meet. It tells them that you belong to Yeshua ha Messiach. In fact, love is more than a simple witness. It is your greatest witness to the world. If this fruit is missing in your life, can you honestly say that you are in the will of God? Can you honestly say that you are living out His purpose and plan for your life? Consider what John was saying about the presence or absence of love in your life.

> *Beloved, let us love one another, for love is of*
> *God; and everyone who loves is born of God and*
> *knows God. He who does not love does not know*
> *God, for God is love.* (1 John 4:7-8)

What are you telling the world by the love you demonstrate through your words and actions? Are you telling the world that you are a disciple of Jesus or that you are just like everyone else? Are you witnessing to others what the power of love can do in and through them? Is the spiritual fruit of love manifesting in your life more and more as time goes by? Think about the consequences of not manifesting this fruit. John is saying that without love people will see that you don't really know God. God is love and so are all His true followers.

2. JOY

Early one morning I was feeling an especially deep level of gratitude to the Lord. He did mighty and awesome things in our presence yesterday, at "The Gathering" in North Wilkesboro, NC. His grace and glory continued to manifest to us on the way home and throughout the evening. This was one of those really awesome times in the presence of the Lord. As I closed my eyes in worship this morning, the Lord gave me a vision which touched me in a very powerful way. I saw the Ark of God coming down from the Temple in Heaven to be in our midst on the Earth. It was surrounded by His fiery Glory like a mighty amber glow of flaming power. I could hear the Heavenly Host singing over and over, *"Now arise, O Lord God, and come to your resting place, you and the ark of your might!"* (2 Chronicles 6:41 and Psalm 132:8) I received a strong witness in my spirit that we are about to experience the manifestation of His Glory as most of us have never seen or experienced it before. It will bring awesome experiences of the Lord's Glory which will change lives forever. I am filled with expectancy and gratitude today. His Glory is getting stronger every day and I can hardly wait for the next outpouring.

Suddenly, I was lifted back to the classroom in Heaven and watched as Jesus raised His hand over each person and released a powerful and life changing blessing. It is very good when someone we respect releases a blessing over us, but it is with overwhelming joy that we receive it directly from the Lord. Then He spoke to us, "Now is a time of blessing! In the way that you receive it, release it to others. There is a great need among my people to receive blessing and favor in this hour." My thoughts went back to Genesis 12:2-3, *"I will make you a great nation; I will bless you and make your name great; and you shall be a blessing. I will bless those who bless you, and I will curse him who curses you; and in you all the families of the earth shall be blessed."* I understood in the Spirit that we have entered again into a season of powerful and transforming blessing, People have heard too much judgment and condemnation, gloom and doom, and angry threats of eternity in Hell. Now, people need to receive the blessing and be loved into the kingdom of God where they can rest in His glory.

As I received and celebrated this blessing from the Lord, I was suddenly carried in the Spirit to another place which looked very familiar. It looked like a larger version of the Upper Room just outside the wall of the Old City in Jerusalem. The giant arches and vaulted ceilings seem to be filled with an air of expectancy for another outpouring of the Holy Spirit. I am so ready for it! How about you? In my spirit I was filled again with expectancy and great joy. I sensed that at any moment the Lord's people would flow into this vast room and a great outpouring of the Spirit would be released. As the disciples needed that power to fulfill their mission, destiny, and purpose given by the Lord, we too have that need right now. I am so hungry for more of His glory, more of His grace, more of His power, and more of His presence! How about you? My spirit and soul went back to a promise from the Lord, *"Blessed are those who hunger and thirst for righteousness, for they shall be filled."* (Matthew 5:6) I want to be filled now! How about you?

I am so thirsty for more of Him and I am standing on the promise of Isaiah 55:1-3, *"Ho! Everyone who thirsts, come to the waters; and you who have no money, come, buy and eat. Yes, come, buy wine and milk without money and without price. Why do you spend money for what is not bread, and your wages for what does not satisfy? Listen carefully to Me, and eat what is good, and let your soul delight itself in abundance. Incline your ear, and come to Me. Hear, and your soul shall live; and I will make an everlasting covenant with you— the sure mercies of David."* I am constantly seeking to be with a group of people as hungry and thirsty as I am to press in together for what the Lord is ready to pour out to us. Join with me as we sincerely cry out to the Lord, *"Now arise, O Lord God, and come to your resting place, you and the ark of your might!"* All I need and all I want in this hour is Him! May He be drawn to us as we draw near to Him with hearts ready to receive whatever He is ready to release to us! Amen and Amen!!!!

ARE YOU IN THE WILL OF GOD?

If you are in the will of God, you will experience God given joy. Have you noticed that many people say they are believers, but there is no joy being manifested in their lives. It is always very sad to see a group of believers who have no apparent joy. How can this be? One primary missions of Yeshua was to release the oil of joy to all who mourn (see Isaiah 61:3). Have you let Yeshua take away every spirit of heaviness in your life? If not, what is holding you back? Let all heaviness go in the name of Jesus. Amen? In full honesty, ask yourself if your life witnesses to others that you have received the oil of joy? This gift of the Lord is the primary source of joy in your life. Don't waste any more time. Go to the Lord and ask Him to anoint you with oil and joy.

*"You love righteousness and hate wickedness;
therefore God, your God, has set you above your
companions by anointing you with the oil of joy."*
(Psalm 45:7)

Obviously this reference is a messianic prophecy. It is also
a prophecy for those who love and serve Yeshua. Read again
what Yeshua said in John 14:12. Think about it. You can do what
He did and even greater things. In all honesty, ask yourself this
question based on the passage above: Do you love righteousness
and hate wickedness? If you answered "Yes" to this question,
you are positioned for an outpouring. Claim the promise and
ask the Lord to release it now and every day. Remember every
promise in the Bible is for you. Seek this blessing in your life.
Ask the Lord to anoint you with the oil of joy to equip you for
your calling.

Joy is very different from happiness. Happiness is an emotion. Happiness is a very limited experience, because it is dependent on your external circumstances. Remember you walk by
faith and not by what you are feeling. Feelings come and go,
but the joy of the Lord is eternal. Joy does its work deep in the
spirit, soul and then in the body. You may be feeling sad. You
may be going through a time of grief. You may have recently
experienced a great loss. Whatever you are feeling, the joy of the
Lord is always available to you. Remember what David said in
Psalm 30:5b, *"Weeping may endure for a night, but joy comes in
the morning."* Be positioned to receive it every morning. I like
to think about it this way: It is always morning somewhere in
the Kingdom of God. I am a citizen of the Kingdom. Therefore,
I can receive this promise anytime I need it. How about you?
Is this promise for you? Then believe that it is always available
and you can be anointed with joy anytime. How about receiving
it right now?

If this fruit is missing, can you truly confess that you are
living fully in the will of God? I don't think so. Think about what

John is saying to you in the following verse: *"And these things we write to you that your joy may be full."* (1 John 1:4) One of the primary purposes of the scriptures is for you to have the fullness of joy. The Lord isn't just telling you to receive a little joy. He isn't offering just enough for you to barely get through the troubles and hardships in your life today. He wants you to have overflowing joy. He wants you to have the fullness of His joy all day every day.

Joy primarily blesses you, and then it overflows to bless others. Paul's teaching lines up precisely with the teachings of Jesus. Notice in the passage below that Jesus encourages you to ask the Father in His Name. This is apparently a new teaching for the disciples. It may seem new to you as well in terms of seeking these specific outcomes. Jesus tells you to ask for whatever you need. Then comes the promise. You will receive it. Then you will receive a very special bonus. Your joy will be full when this happens.

> *And in that day you will ask Me nothing. Most assuredly, I say to you, whatever you ask the Father in My name He will give you. Until now you have asked nothing in My name. Ask, and you will receive, that your joy may be full.* (John 16:23-24)

Have you ever been around someone who truly exudes joy? If you have, I am certain that it was a wonderful experience for you? I like joy filled people. I love those who overflow with joy in a way which also blesses others. Gloria and I have a friend named, Ken Peltier, who manifests this fruit of the Spirit more than anyone else we know. It is such a joy to be around him, and the Lord uses him in amazing ways to bless others. No matter what he is going through in life, joy just keeps bubbling forth from him. Ministering to other people and praying for them gives him profound joy and produces fruit in the lives of everyone around him. Would you like to be like that? You can. It is a gift from the Lord and He wants to bless you with an over-flow. Consider what Peter is saying in the passage below:

> *In this you greatly rejoice, though now for a little while, if need be, you have been grieved by various trials, that the genuineness of your faith, being much more precious than gold that perishes, though it is tested by fire, may be found to praise, honor, and glory at the revelation of Jesus Christ, whom having not seen you love. Though now you do not see Him, yet believing, you rejoice with **joy inexpressible** and full of glory, receiving the end of your faith—the salvation of your souls.* (1 Peter 1:6-9)

The night of grief is over for believers. Joy has come in place of heaviness and sadness. As Peter says, this is a time to "greatly rejoice." Your faith has been demonstrated in the midst of trials, temptations, and hardships. You have been tested by fire, but then you were enabled to give praise, honor and glory to the Lord. You have been able to do this because of the revelation of Yeshua ha Messiach. The end result of staying faithful during these tough times is the "joy inexpressible and full of glory" which follows. Hallelujah! Thank you Lord! Amen and Amen!

3. PEACE

> *For "He who would love life and see good days, let him refrain his tongue from evil, and his lips from speaking deceit. Let him turn away from evil and do good; let him **seek peace and pursue it**. For the eyes of the LORD are on the righteous, and His ears are open to their prayers; but the face of the LORD is against those who do evil."* (1 Peter 3:10-12)

Do you want to please the Lord? His eyes are always on those who are righteous in His sight. Are you one of the righteous? Peter's advice is very important for us to accept in the depth of our being. Take a moment to examine your own life. Do you seek peace? Do you pursue His Shalom? Peter says that the Lord is very attentive to the prayers of those who seek peace. If your prayers don't seem to produce the results you desire, perhaps this is the key for you to open the door of breakthrough. I'm just saying…! Receive this powerful promise: *"His ears are open to their prayers."* Now claim it for yourself by saying: "His ears are open to my prayers."

Peace comes to those who are in the will of God. Consider carefully what James says about peace in James 3:18, *"Now the fruit of righteousness is sown in peace by those who make peace."* This is like a double portion fruit of the Spirit. Those who truly bring peace sow it as a fruit of righteousness. Then it produces a spiritual crop. Peace produces more peace. Like Peter said in 1 Peter 1:2b, *"Grace to you and peace be multiplied."* This is Kingdom math. It is not as much about adding as it is about multiplying the fruit in your life.

Peace is one of the gifts of the Lord which He loves to multiply for you. I am praying for that right now. Lord, please let peace multiply in all our lives and in our ministries. Give us an overflow in this area so that we can also sow seeds of peace in the lives of others. Please open the Floodgates of Heaven and pour out more than we can contain so that it will overflow to others. Put your faith behind the prayer. Believe it. Receive it and give thanks for it today and every day.

The Lord's peace is above and beyond what we are able to understand with our limited powers of reasoning. Consider what Paul says in Philippians 4:7 (NIV), *"And the peace of God, which **transcends all understanding**, will guard your hearts and your minds in Christ Jesus."* The Hebrew word translated as peace is "Shalom." As I shared earlier, the "Shalom" of God is actually much more than peace. It essentially means that through the Lord's provision you have all that you need in every area of your life. This is real peace. This is the "Shalom" of God.

Shalom is like the seven-fold blessing of righteous Abraham. When you have all you need, you will experience it as a deep sense of peace and trust in the Lord. As I mentioned earlier, I like to break this seven-fold blessing down as peace, provision, protection, prosperity, productivity, power and prophetic words. I speak this every day because I want all this to manifest in my life and ministry. How about you? Are you confessing these things daily? Remember, this is the blessing of the Lord for those who live by the spirit of righteousness.

Biblical peace most directly means peace with God. Every other type of peace is subordinate to this peace. In Romans 5:1, Paul wrote, *"Therefore, since we have been justified through faith, we have **peace with God** through our Lord Jesus Christ,"* In other words, we are no longer enemies, because the Lord has established peace in our lives and in our relationship with Him. You can see this clearly in the teaching of Paul in Romans 5:8, *"But God demonstrates His own love toward us, in that while we were still sinners, Christ died for us."* If the fruit of peace is missing in your life and ministry, can you honestly say that you are in the will of God?

Who are you in Jesus Christs? Listen to what Peter says about that in 1 Peter 2:9, *"But you are a chosen generation, a royal priesthood, a holy nation, His own special people, that you may proclaim the praises of Him who called you out of darkness into His marvelous light;"* Claim it all for yourself. Declare and decree who you are. You have been chosen by the Lord to live in this time and to accomplish His purposes for the advancement of the Kingdom of God. You were chosen to be part of a royal priesthood to administer the promises of the Lord in your generation. You are part of a holy nation, because your citizenship in in Heaven. You are special. Don't let the enemy take that away from you! Amen?

PRAYER

Father God,
I want to be a consecrated and faithful disciple of Jesus Christ.
I covenant to go where you tell me to go;
to do what you want me to do;
to say what you tell me to say;
and to be led by the Holy Spirit every step of the way.

Father, I submit my life to you as a disciple in the service of Jesus Christ.

Here am I Lord! Send me! This I pray in Jesus' name. Amen!

*Grace to you and **peace** from Him who is and who was and who is to come, and from the seven Spirits who are before His throne, and from Jesus Christ, the faithful witness, the firstborn from the dead, and the ruler over the kings of the earth.*
(Revelation 1:4b-5)

Chapter Five

VISIBLE IN FRUIT FOR OTHERS

I had a very unusual experience with the Lord this morning. After spending time in the Word and in worship, I felt myself being lifted up to Heaven through something like a tunnel made of a protective membrane. I traveled through the second heaven completely protected by the material around the tunnel. Finally, I sort of popped out of the tunnel and landed on my feet on the top of Revelation Mountain. I expected some wonderful encounter with the Lord and looked forward to spending time with Him. However, that didn't happen. As I stood on the mountain, I went into an open vision in which I was allowed to watch someone going out of their way to be exceptionally helpful to a stranger. Before I could get any wisdom about this, it was over and I was on the floor in the worship room. To be completely honest, I thought that perhaps I had done something wrong which caused the visit to end so abruptly.

Before I could think through this experience, I was back in the tunnel moving quickly toward Heaven. Once again I popped out of the tunnel and landed on my feet about 50 feet from the opening. I was on Revelation Mountain again, and filled with expectancy. Then I went into another open vision. I was standing near someone in another country watching them do some very extraordinary things to help others in need. The person receiving the assistance did not appear to be very grateful, but it didn't deter the one giving assistance. Before I could think more about this, I was back in the worship room, face down on the floor with something tickling the side of my head. I brushed it away and was immediately lifted up through the tunnel again. This process happened over and over. Each time, I was in a different part of the world standing with people who were ministering to others. I watched as people were healed, delivered, blessed, fed, taught, and led by these selfless servants of Jesus Christ. They were doing all these things without reward or even a modest demonstrations of appreciation. Yet, they persisted, because they were doing it for the Lord.

I thought about what Jesus said in Matthew 25:37-40, *"Then the righteous will answer Him, saying, 'Lord, when did we see You hungry and feed You, or thirsty and give You drink? When did we see You a stranger and take You in, or naked and clothe You? Or when did we see You sick, or in prison, and come to You?' And the King will answer and say to them, 'Assuredly, I say to you, inasmuch as you did it to one of the least of these My brethren, you did it to Me.'"* All of the people I had seen were like these righteous ones who did it because it was in their nature and character as those transformed by the Lord. Are you one of these?

The final visit to Heaven this morning proceeded just like the others except I didn't have an open vision. As I stood on Revelation Mountain, I heard the Lord say, "This is a day for extraordinary acts of kindness! This will be a more powerful witness than any of your persuasive words or carefully crafted programs! Today, you are extremely blessed to be an extraordinary blessing to others!"

Lord, please change our character and nature so that we are more like you and the righteous ones you showed me today! Please give us a servant heart so that we can bless others as you have blessed us! Freely we have received, help us to freely give today and always! May we please and bless the Lord today by our humble obedience! Amen and Amen!

BECOMING WHO YOU ARE IN CHRIST

It is a good thing to know who you are in Christ, but that doesn't take you far enough. Unless you put it into action, it will be unfruitful knowledge. It is good to have faith in the words of Yeshua which tell you who you are, but more is still needed. Think about the teaching in James 2:20 (KJV), *"But wilt thou know, O vain man, that faith without works is dead?"* It is one thing to know who you are, but it is another thing to become who you are in Christ. This kind of becoming is a lifelong process. I see it as an exciting adventure of discovery and fulfillment as you work side by side with the Lord to live out your amazing God given and God ordained destiny.

The purpose of this book is to assist you in the process of discovering and becoming exactly who you were created, anointed, and gifted to be. One of the purposes of your seer anointing is for the Lord to reveal this to you. Then you can see the pattern of your calling as Moses saw the pattern for the Tabernacle on the Holy Mountain. Again this is one of the purposes of your seer anointing, but it is not the only way the Lord reveals His plans to you. As you move forward in accomplishing your divine purpose, the Lord gives you confirmations along the way that you are on the right path. One of the ways you know that you are on the right track, is by the spiritual fruit in your life.

> *But the fruit of the Spirit is love, joy, peace, long-suffering, kindness, goodness, faithfulness, gentleness, self-control. Against such there is no law. And those who are Christ's have crucified the flesh with its passions and desires. If we live in the Spirit, let us also walk in the Spirit. Let*

us not become conceited, provoking one another, envying one another. (Galatians 5:22-26)

HOW DO YOU KNOW IF YOU ARE IN THE WILL OF GOD?

For a good tree does not bear bad fruit, nor does a bad tree bear good fruit. For every tree is known by its own fruit. For men do not gather figs from thorns, nor do they gather grapes from a bramble bush. A good man out of the good treasure of his heart brings forth good; and an evil man out of the evil treasure of his heart brings forth evil. For out of the abundance of the heart his mouth speaks. (Luke 6:43-45)

Consider the spiritual fruit being produced in your life and through your service for the Lord. Is it good fruit? If not, what do you need to do about it? The Lord is always gracious and merciful to those who turn to Him in repentance. He is in the restoration business and would love the opportunity to help you have a more fruitful life. He wants to bless you so that you can be a blessing to others. This is a part of your inheritance. If you need to improve your relationship with the Lord, begin right now. Don't put it off any longer. He is ready and willing to restore you and return you to the paths of righteousness.

On the other hand, if you see good spiritual fruit flowing from your life and work, it is a good time to give thanks to the Lord for what He is accomplishing through you. Begin to seek ways to produce even more of this good fruit. Remember: the Lord is in the business of multiplication and increase. I often release a prayer of David over those who have been called for service in the Kingdom. I pray this prayer from Psalm 115:14-15 over you now: "*May the Lord give you increase more and more, you and your children. May you be blessed by the Lord, Who made heaven and earth.*" As you focus on the fruit you are producing for others, perhaps you can begin to release this blessing over others as well.

When Father God releases to you the blessing of Abraham, you will produce real spiritual fruit. You will be a blessing to others through this fruit. Think about it. Claim the promise in Genesis 12:2b-3, "*I will bless you and make your name great; and you shall be a blessing. I will bless those who bless you, and I will curse him who curses you; and in you all the families of the earth shall be blessed.*" This is Abraham's blessing which comes to you through the work of Jesus. You are an heir to this promise. You have a great purpose and destiny in the kingdom of God. The Lord has called you to be a partner with Him in the blessing business. Now is the time for that spiritual fruit to manifest and flourish.

FRUIT INTO THE LIVES OF OTHERS

1. LONGSUFFERING

Now the Lord descended in the cloud and stood with him there, and proclaimed the name of the Lord. And the Lord passed before him and proclaimed, "The Lord, the Lord God, merciful and gracious, longsuffering, and abounding in goodness and truth, keeping mercy for thousands, forgiving iniquity and transgression and sin, by no means clearing the guilty, visiting the iniquity of the fathers upon the children and the children's children to the third and the fourth generation." (Exodus 34:5-7)

When the Lord met with Moses on Mount Sinai, He gave the greatest self-revelation of His personality ever released to anyone in all of human history. Moses received this revelation on the mountain and passed it on to you and me. This is a keystone moment in our relationship with the Lord and we do well to understand it fully. In the passage above, the Lord gives Moses an understanding of His thirteen primary attributes. These attributes are listed in Appendix One at the end of the book. I recommend that you pause at this point to look at the details of this revelation.

Many people read this story without fully taking in the powerful message being released through it. Do you want to know God better? Study His meeting with Moses on Mount Sinai and fully embrace all of His powerful and wonderful attributes. Try to put yourself into this situation. Visualize yourself there on the mountain with Moses meeting the Lord and receiving this amazing and wonderful understanding of the true nature of the Lord. Notice the Lord is revealing the fact that we can know Him best by understanding the spiritual fruit He is releasing to us. Think about that. You were created in His image and you reveal who you are by the spiritual fruit you release to others.

After considering this carefully, study the life, works and words of Yeshua ha Messiach and see how He manifested these same attributes. Remember that He is the same yesterday, today and forever. This is who He is and who He is calling you to be. As you go from glory to glory (2 Corinthians 3:18, *"But we all, with unveiled face, beholding as in a mirror the glory of the Lord, are being transformed into the same image from glory to glory, just as by the Spirit of the Lord."*), you are becoming more like Him. You are being transformed as you grow into His image. You are beginning to possess the same attributes. Wow! That is such an awesome thought.

Moses asked to see the Lord's glory, and the Lord said He would show Moses His goodness. All of these thirteen attributes are part of the Lord's goodness even if you do not fully understand how they work. For example: how is it the goodness of the Lord to visit the iniquity of the fathers on the children into the fourth generation? It is difficult to understand this. Theologians have struggled with this throughout the centuries. Sometimes you must take it on faith that the Lord is working something good in your life no matter how it looks or feels. I like the way this is translated in the "Complete Jewish Bible" (CJB), *"showing grace to the thousandth generation, forgiving offenses, crimes and sins; yet not exonerating the guilty, but causing the negative effects of the parent's offenses to be experienced by their children and grandchildren, and even by the third and fourth generations."* (Exodus 34:7) I believe these negative effects are revealed by God's mercy so that the following generation will learn not to make the same mistakes.

Before you attempt to judge these attributes, it is important to realize that some of them go beyond your ability to understand. Notice that one of the Lord's attributes is "longsuffering." He does not visit judgment on people quickly or capriciously. He suffers for a long time before making a decision that judgment is the only way to bring people to a saving knowledge of who He is. Without judgment, people would begin to question His fairness toward those being hurt in the process. Why would the Lord let a wicked person continue to harm people year after year? At some point, the Lord's goodness has to be shown toward those being injured by a wicked person. Then His judgment manifests.

The fact is that negative things seem to get passed from one generation to another. The wickedness of a father is often transferred within the family culture to the next generation. Unless the Lord intervenes to stop the chain of pain, it just keeps recurring. We need to see that the Lord's judgments come to call people into repentance so they can be restored to their God-given purpose in life. This requires more longsuffering than most people can produce. Therefore, longsuffering is a spiritual gift and the fruit of it is actually something supernatural in our world. Let the Lord do a supernatural work through you by increasing your ability to produce the spiritual fruit of longsuffering. This too is a lifelong process. You need to begin as soon as possible to let the Holy Spirit release this spiritual fruit through you to others who have been given into your care and in your service for the Lord.

Remember you were created in God's image and His thirteen attributes of goodness should be manifesting in your life. If you are in the will of God, you will learn to be a patient person. In other words, you too will become longsuffering in your relationships with others. You will be patient and endure many painful experiences as you pray and wait on the Lord to bring transformation in their lives. Sometimes while you are practicing longsuffering, you come to realize the source of the problem in your relationships is from within you rather than the other persons.

I take great assurance in what the Word of God says about our Lord. Right now you can receive the promise of the Lord given through Jeremiah in Lamentations 3:22-23, *"Through the Lord's mercies we are not consumed, because His compassions fail not. They are new every morning; great is Your faithfulness. "The Lord is my portion," says my soul, "Therefore I hope in Him!"* No matter what you are going through, you can count on the Lord's mercy and grace. It is important to be certain about this when you go through seasons of admonishment and discipline. Whatever challenge you may face, you will always have His faithfulness. It often comes in waves of glory so that it seems to be new every morning. Be encouraged to honestly search out areas where you need to improve. The Lord will bless you as you do this.

Most people are not able to clearly see their own shortcomings. They are much better at seeing faults in others. It takes another supernatural work of the Holy Spirit to enable you to see your own shortcomings. It is so important for this work to be done in your walk with the Lord. Otherwise, you may think you are doing very well when in reality you are failing at your primary mission. This is why the Lord gave us a principle to follow in Luke 6:43-44, *"For a good tree does not bear bad fruit, nor does a bad tree bear good fruit. For every tree is known by its own fruit. For men do not gather figs from thorns, nor do they gather grapes from a bramble bush."* You can know yourself by the fruit flowing through you.

What do you do if the spiritual fruit in your life doesn't seem to match up with the Lord's standards? I constantly ask the Lord to admonish and disciple me quickly when I need it. He has always been so good to answer this prayer. It doesn't always feel good, but it is necessary if you are going to constantly improve the way you walk with Him. Every time the Lord admonishes you, it is an opportunity for you to repent and get back on the righteous path He has laid out for you. Each time you go through this process, you will be enabled to produce more of the spiritual fruit of longsuffering. You will be given the opportunity to continuously grow in your relationships with others as well as with the Lord.

Patient longsuffering, is the character of a true disciple. Paul instructs his spiritual son to be a more effective minister in 2 Timothy 4:2, *"Preach the word! Be ready in season and out of season. Convince, rebuke, exhort, with all **longsuffering** and teaching."* Without the fruit of longsuffering, most people will be too impatient to allow others time to change. For most people, you will notice that as impatience begins to manifest, the focus of their conversations will often shift toward increasing the flow of words of rebuke. When this happens, their relationships with others can be damaged and the desired outcome will not be produced. Paul had to learn this by personal experience. This is usually true of all of us. It is much less painful to learn this from Paul's experience rather than your own. In the passage below, let his learning experiences be a guide for your development.

I, therefore, the prisoner of the Lord, beseech you
to walk worthy of the calling with which you were
called, with all lowliness and gentleness, with

longsuffering, bearing with one another in love, endeavoring to keep the unity of the Spirit in the bond of peace. (Ephesians 4:1-3)

Effective disciples have learned not to be ruled by offenses. Consider what Solomon taught in Proverbs 20:3, *"It is honorable for a man to stop striving, since any fool can start a quarrel."* True disciples prefer to bear the offense rather than to get into strife. When you get into strife, you are likely to give an offense to the other person. When this happens, that person will likely strike out and increase the offense in you. Someone has to break the chain of pain. If you are a disciple of Jesus Christ, He has called you to be that person. Think about it. If this fruit is missing in your life and work, can you truly say that you are in the will of God? I want to end this section on the spiritual fruit of longsuffering by sharing a prayer from Psalm 130. You always have the promise from the Lord of forgiveness and restoration.

If you, O LORD, kept a record of sins, O Lord, who could stand? But with you there is forgiveness; therefore you are feared. I wait for the LORD, my soul waits, and in his word I put my hope. My soul waits for the Lord more than watchmen wait for the morning, more than watchmen wait for the morning. (Psalm 130:3-6)

2. KINDNESS

Therefore, as the elect of God, holy and beloved, put on tender mercies, kindness, humility, meekness, longsuffering; bearing with one another, and forgiving one another, if anyone has a complaint against another; even as Christ forgave you, so you also must do." (Colossians 3:12-13)

What kind of person are you? Do other people often comment about the kindness you show in your relationships with them and others? Sometimes you can get a better picture of your spiritual fruit through the eyes of others than you own. Be aware that you may get more truth this way than you desire. This is why many people avoid hearing what others are saying about them. When it comes to spiritual fruit, it is a good thing to go through times of self-examination. It is easy to overlook your own shortcomings while keeping a close watch on others.

The spiritual fruit of kindness is very important in the Kingdom of God. It seems strange that in many groups of believers this fruit seems woefully lacking. How much of their witness has been diminished by the lack of kindness? In the passage below, notice the power of kindness. The kindness of the Lord has worked miracles in our lives. Our salvation is due in large part to the kindness of the Lord. Think about it. Where would you be without the kindness of the Lord?

> *But when the kindness and the love of God our Savior toward man appeared, not by works of righteousness which we have done, but according to His mercy He saved us, through the washing of regeneration and renewing of the Holy Spirit, whom He poured out on us abundantly through Jesus Christ our Savior, that having been justified by His grace we should become heirs according to the hope of eternal life.* (Titus 3:4-7)

Created in the image of God, your spiritual attributes should be like His. Is this true in your life? If His kindness brought about such a powerful transition in all believers, what will it do for others through you? Think about it. What if other people could see the kindness of the Lord in your life? What impact could that have on them? I believe it would cause your evangelistic work to become much easier because people would naturally be open to hearing your testimony. Kindness is a very powerful spiritual force. I think it is one of the secret weapons of our spiritual warfare. Think about it as you read the passage below.

> *For the weapons of our warfare are not carnal but mighty in God for pulling down strongholds, casting down arguments and every high thing that exalts itself against the knowledge of God, bringing every thought into captivity to the obedience of Christ, and being ready to punish all disobedience when your obedience is fulfilled.* (2 Corinthians 10:4-6)

You have a secret weapon. It is so subtle and so pleasant that people are really open to let it do the work of the Spirit. Your kindness can bring down strongholds. It can cast down arguments and open doors of opportunity in your relationship with others. It can bring the thoughts of others into captivity so that the Gospel of the Kingdom can do a mighty work in their lives. This is true Godly kindness and it was meant as a gift for you. It was a gift to bring you to salvation, and it is a gift to flow through you to bring others into the Kingdom of God. It is amazing and wonderful.

If the spiritual fruit of kindness is flowing in you, it is a strong indicator that you are in the will of God. When this fruit manifests, it means much more than just being kind to the beautiful and nice people around you. You need to go beyond this and be kind to those who may not seem to deserve it by worldly standards. It is not easy to administer kindness when your heart feels like rebuking the other person. It is the mark of a true disciple who can do what he sees Jesus doing and say what he hears Jesus saying.

To be an effective disciple of Yeshua ha Messiach, you must begin to intentionally practice kindness. Keep it up until it becomes your nature. Then it will become so natural that it will flow easily and manifest constantly. This will not likely happen overnight. This is another place for persistence to manifest. Think about what Paul is teaching in the passage below:

> *We give no offense in anything, that our ministry may not be blamed. But in all things we commend ourselves as ministers of God: in much patience, in tribulations, in needs, in distresses, in stripes, in imprisonments, in tumults, in labors, in sleeplessness, in fastings; by purity, by knowledge, by longsuffering, by kindness, by the Holy Spirit, by sincere love, by the word of truth, by the power of God, by the armor of righteousness on the right hand and on the left, by honor and dishonor, by evil report and good report; as deceivers, and yet true; as unknown, and yet well known; as dying, and behold we live; as chastened, and yet not killed; as sorrowful, yet always rejoicing; as poor, yet making many rich; as having nothing, and yet possessing all things.* (2 Corinthians 6:3-10)

Several years ago, I met a man who wanted to do NASCAR ministry. When I heard this, I jumped to an incorrect assumption. I had ministered in a Hospital close to a race track. This track was for horse racing. In my job as a hospital chaplain, I had many opportunities to minister to injured riders, trainers and other laborers. From my experience, I started to talk to this man about pit crews, track maintenance people, and those who worked on small details. As I talked with him, I used my example of ministering to jockeys, trainers, and those who assisted them. The man quickly corrected me. He didn't have any desire for that type of ministry.

He wanted to associate with and minister to the famous drivers and the celebrities who gather around them. He seemed to have a need to elevate himself into the realm of these celebrities. I was stunned by this unexpected outcome. I had to pause and look at myself. Was I ministering to others out of kindness or making an attempt to elevate myself. I recommend this process of continuously examining yourself to see if you minister kindness from a pure heart. As you do this, you may need to do some spiritual house cleaning. I really like the way The Message Bible deals with the passage below.

So clean house! Make a clean sweep of malice and pretense, envy and hurtful talk. You've had a taste of God. Now, like infants at the breast, drink deep of God's pure kindness. Then you'll grow up mature and whole in God. (1 Peter2:1-3, TMSG)

I believe that true disciples of Yeshua ha Messiach will be characterized by kindness toward those who don't deserve it by worldly standards. This is the Lord's type of kindness. He was kind toward us when we didn't deserve it. While we were still His enemies, He sent Jesus to do a work of great kindness in us. We are called to minister as Jesus ministered; with the spiritual gift of kindness at work in and through us. When we do it His way, we are in the process of bringing others to Him. We are also bringing the part of Him which resides in us to them. Ask yourself a question. If this fruit is missing, are you actually in the will of God?

3. GENTLENESS

Gentleness is the fruit of a life fully committed to God. Paul instructs the church in Philippians 4:5, *"Let your gentleness be known to all men. The Lord is at hand."* Paul gives us a powerful reason to demonstrate this attribute of the Lord. He is returning soon and we will have to account for how we treated His other sons and daughters when He arrives. How can you explain or justify a lack of gentleness in your contact with others? How will you explain giving a poor witness for the Lord in your daily behavior?

> *For He will deliver the needy when he cries, the poor also, and him who has no helper. He will spare the poor and needy, and will save the souls of the needy. He will redeem their life from oppression and violence; and precious shall be their blood in His sight.* (Psalm 72:12-14)

If you want to please the Lord, touch every life as if it is a fragile and beautiful work of the Lord's artistic creativity, because each life is just that. Always remember that those who are not highly valued in the world are precious in His sight. We must never forget the value of others to Him. We are called to be gentle with all people. Think about how the gentleness of the Lord has blessed you. David said it very well in Psalm 18:35-36, "*You have also given me the shield of Your salvation; Your right hand has held me up, Your gentleness has made me great. You enlarged my path under me, so my feet did not slip.*" His gentleness has made you great. This is an awesome spiritual gift the Lord has given to you.

There is great power in gentleness. Only truly powerful people can interact with others in gentleness. It is a sign of how much spiritual authority and power the Lord releases to you and through you with the spiritual fruit of gentleness. Look again at the basic passage of scripture used to introduce this topic. This time with the focus on the gift of gentleness, notice what it is saying about you. If you have crucified the flesh, there is no longer any worldly offense which can touch you. You have risen above it. The Lord has made no law against these powerful spiritual fruits because they are among His primary attributes. He created you to live and minister this same way.

But the fruit of the Spirit is love, joy, peace, long-suffering, kindness, goodness, faithfulness, gentleness, self-control. Against such there is no law. And those who are Christ's have crucified the flesh with its passions and desires. If we live in the Spirit, let us also walk in the Spirit. (Galatians 5:22-25)

When you produce these fruits, you will be living a life which is pleasing to the Lord. As disciples, we are called to be especially gentle with those most fragile in the view of the flesh. Only a truly strong person can afford to be gentle with those who do not seem worthy of it. This kind of gifted person is living on a spiritual level so far above those still in the world that it will be a mystery to them. They will not understand your strength reflected in your gentleness, but they will certainly feel it. If you have a heart for evangelism, be intentional about ministering with this spiritual fruit. You are impacting eternity when you win the lost for the Lord. What greater sense of accomplishment could you desire?

And a servant of the Lord must not quarrel but be gentle to all, able to teach, patient, in humility correcting those who are in opposition, if God perhaps will grant them repentance, so that they may know the truth, and that they may come to their senses and escape the snare of the devil, having been taken captive by him to do his will. (2 Timothy 2:24-26)

You must always remember that others are precious in His sight. When you are gentle with them, you will be able to teach them. No one ever said that this would be easy. That is why it is such a powerful witness to your spiritual strength. This type of ministry takes great patience. When correction is needed in others, you must give it with love and gentleness so that person can accept it. This is necessary so others can receive it without being humiliated before those around them. Remember that the Lord does not will for anyone to be abused. Think about it! If this fruit is missing, can you truly say that you are in the will of the Father, the Son and the Holy Spirit?

*For the love of money is a root of all kinds of evil, for which some have strayed from the faith in their greediness, and pierced themselves through with many sorrows. But you, man of God, flee from all this, and pursue righteousness, godliness, faith, love, endurance and **gentleness**. Fight the good fight of the faith. Take hold of the eternal life to which you were called when you made your good confession in the presence of many witnesses.* (1 Timothy 6:10-12)

YOU CAN ABSOLUTELY KNOW
IF YOU'RE IN THE WILL OF GOD

And this I pray, that your love may abound still more and more in knowledge and all discernment, that you may approve the things that are excellent, that you may be sincere and without offense till the day of Christ, being filled with the fruits of righteousness which are by Jesus Christ, to the glory and praise of God. (Philippians 1:9-11)

Think about the joy of being without offense on the day of Christ's return. I don't want to be offended by Him and I do not want to offend Him. How about you? Will the fruit in your life please Him or offend Him? That is the question you need to face now rather than on that day. It is not too late. You can repent and return to living in the will of Father God. He has made it simple and easy for you, however it cannot be in word only. It must be reflected in a positive change in your fruit bearing.

Therefore bear fruits worthy of repentance, and do not begin to say to yourselves, "We have Abraham as our father." For I say to you that God is able to raise up children to Abraham from these stones. And even now the ax is laid to the root of the trees. Therefore every tree which does not bear good fruit is cut down and thrown into the fire. (Luke 3:8-9)

Think about it! The presence of the "fruit of the Spirit" proves that your repentance is genuine. You are living in a wonderful time of grace and you receive it based on your genuine and sincere repentance. You need to have a spirit of repentance like Daniel exhibited in Daniel 9:3-7. Like Daniel, you need to repent for your nation, state, city, church and neighborhood. As citizens of a nation or members of a community we are partially responsible for their actions even if we didn't personally sin. Repentance has to start with someone. Why not you and me?

The Word of God teaches us to bear fruit worthy of repentance. You are to produce "fruit" that demonstrates the depth of your sincerity. Too often, people think all these things are tasks for someone else. In this season, the Lord is calling on us to be the ones who will build a wall and stand in the gap so that judgment may stop and grace, mercy and peace may flow through. It is your honor and privilege to be that person in this generation. It is your blessing to be allowed to do this great work of the Lord.

God's will: for "flesh driven" people is for them to become "Spirit driven" disciples. Paul expressed it well in Galatians 5:24-25, "*And those who are Christ's have crucified the flesh with its passions and desires. If we live in the Spirit, let us also walk in the Spirit.*" The Lord wants more than pious words and empty affirmations. He desires for you to put all these things into action. His will for you is that your spiritual attributes will daily become more like His attributes. Look again at those attributes listed in Exodus 34:5-7 (and in Appendix One), and begin to intentionally model this in your life and work for the Kingdom of God.

Make it your practice to daily consecrate yourself to the covenant made for you through the work of Yeshua ha Messiach! You will be known by the spiritual fruit in your life which blesses others. You will be able to see it and others will know it through their experience with you. You may need to open your spiritual eyes to truly see the depth of the Lord's calling in your life. Let you seer anointing be released now to show you how far and how high the Lord wants to take you in the fulfillment of your Kingdom destiny.

PRAYER OF CONSECRATION

Father God,

I want to be a consecrated and faithful disciple of Jesus Christ. I covenant to do my best to bear fruit in the lives of others. Help me to flow with longsuffering, gentleness and kindness toward your other children. Help me to be a blessing in the lives of all those I meet and work with in fulfilling my purpose for you. Teach me to say what I hear you saying and to manifest your attributes in my ministry. I ask you to let me be led by the Holy Spirit every step of the way. Father, I submit my life to you as a disciple in the service of Jesus Christ. Here am I! Send me! This I pray in Jesus' name. Amen!

By this My Father is glorified, that you bear much fruit; so you will be My disciples. (John 15:8)

Chapter Six

VISIBLE IN FRUIT
FOR THE LORD

This morning as I entered into His presence I was seeking the peace and rest of Shabbat. This is a special Shabbat because it is also Rosh Chodesh – a day to give first fruit offerings. I gave myself to the Lord as a first fruit offering this morning. In my spirit, I became aware that I am the first born son in my family and I belong to the Lord. This felt right and I pressed in for what the Lord has promised to those who commit to Him. Then I heard Him say, "Don't cry out for it! Don't strive for it! Don't press in for it! This is a day of rest. Rest in Me and wait in faith for Me to provide for you!' My thoughts went to the passages of scripture where we have been told to "wait on the Lord."

First, I thought of Isaiah 40:31, *"But those who wait on the Lord Shall renew their strength; They shall mount up with wings like eagles, They shall run and not be weary, They shall walk and not faint."* If we wait on the Lord, we "Shall renew" our strength! I was grateful for the capital "S" on the word "Shall." This is a statement of faith, and the Lord said for us to wait in faith and know that He "Shall" keep His promises to us! Amen?

Then two other passages about waiting on the Lord were given to me. Psalm 27:14, *"Wait on the Lord; be of good courage, and He shall strengthen your heart; Wait, I say, on the Lord!*" Psalm 37:34, "*Wait on the Lord, and keep His way, and He shall exalt you to inherit the land; when the wicked are cut off, you shall see it.*" How many of us really do this? Do we wait on the Lord or continue to press in and seek things more fervently? There is a time to press in and strive for the things of the Lord, but today is not that day. Today is a day of rest, refreshing, renewing, and patient trust in the Lord. Are we able to do that?

I pray that we are able, willing, and ready to follow what the Lord has given us! I pray that we will trust Him to provide good and perfect gifts for us without us having to continually beg for them. Remember James 1:16-18, "*Do not be deceived, my beloved brethren. Every good gift and every perfect gift is from above, and comes down from the Father of lights, with whom there is no variation or shadow of turning. Of His own will He brought us forth by the word of truth, that we might be a kind of firstfruits of His creatures.*" Good and perfect gifts are part of His plan for us and His promise for us! This is the time to wait in faith for the manifestation of these promises. Did you notice the last part of that passage? We are all "a kind of first-fruits of His creatures." We are the first-fruit offering to the Lord today and our patience in waiting on Him will demonstrate our faith in His promises. I pray that all these blessings will manifest through Yeshua ha Messiach. Amen and Amen!

SEEING YOUR BLIND SPOT

Everyone, to some decree, has a blind spot about their own personality and performance. Some things are visible to others and you can get feedback from them if you are mature enough to accept it. You can evaluate your ability to receive correction in accordance with Proverbs 9:8, "*Do not correct a scoffer, lest he hate you; rebuke a wise man, and he will love you.*" If you tend to hate those who point out your shortcomings, you might be a "scoffer." If you love those who tell you the truth about yourself, you are probably a very wise person. If by this test you are a wise person, receive the blessing which follows in Proverbs 9:9, *"Give instruction to a wise man, and he will be still wiser; teach a just man, and he will increase in learning."* If you are reading this, I believe you are a wise person willing to receive instruction, correction and insight.

I also believe that there are areas in your blind spot which are known only to the Lord. If you are to improve in these areas, you need help from the Lord. This is one of the reasons the Lord released the seer anointing on the Day of Pentecost. Remember this anointing is available to all flesh. Some people don't want it. Others don't believe it is possible. What do you think? It is a good time to speak to your spirit again and command it to awaken your spiritual eyes and ears to see and hear what the Lord wants you to know. One of the ways you know whether you need this help or not is to examine yourself to see if the fruit of the Spirit is manifesting in your life and work. Look again at the cornerstone passage about spiritual fruit and ask the Lord to reveal what you need to see right now.

> *But the fruit of the Spirit is love, joy, peace, long-suffering, kindness, goodness, faithfulness, gentleness, self-control. Against such there is no law. And those who are Christ's have crucified the flesh with its passions and desires. If we live in the Spirit, let us also walk in the Spirit. Let us not become conceited, provoking one another, envying one another.* (Galatians 5:22-26)

In each of the previous chapters, I attempted to answer the question: how do you know if you are in the will of God? How are you doing so far? This is a very important question if you want to do the things which please the Lord. If you need to make changes, it is better to find out now. It is far better to repent and seek to return than to try to explain failures when the Lord returns. Remember what Jesus said about this.

> *But why do you call Me 'Lord, Lord,' and not do the things which I say? Whoever comes to Me, and hears My sayings and does them, I will show you whom he is like: He is like a man building a house, who dug deep and laid the foundation on the rock. And when the flood arose, the stream beat vehemently against that house, and could not shake it, for it was founded on the rock. But he who heard and did nothing is like a man who built a house on the earth without a foundation, against which the stream beat vehemently; and immediately it fell. And the ruin of that house was great.* (Luke 6:46-49)

A servant strives to please his master. An athlete seeks to conform to the rules and please the judges in order to win in competition. How can anyone believe it is okay to do less in their relationship with the Lord? Are you producing spiritual fruit which pleases the Lord? Paul reminded Timothy that a soldier on active duty seeks to please his or her commander. Should we expect to do less with the Lord?

> *No one serving as a soldier gets involved in civilian affairs—he wants to please his commanding officer. Similarly, if anyone competes as an athlete, he does not receive the victor's crown unless he competes according to the rules.* (2 Timothy 2:4-5)

There are spiritual rules set up by the Lord and we will be judged according to how we obey them. I am going to bring up something which is very controversial. You can decide for yourself how you view the next series of Biblical teachings. Many people no longer believe there will be any judgment for believers. What do you think? Listen to what the Lord says in, Matthew 12:36-37, *"But I say to you that for every idle word men may speak, they will give account of it in the day of judgment. For by your words you will be justified, and by your words you will be condemned."* Paul drew a conclusion about this in his letter to the church in Corinth.

> *Therefore we make it our aim, whether present or absent, to be well pleasing to Him. For we must all appear before the judgment seat of Christ, that each one may receive the things done in the body, according to what he has done, whether good or bad.* (2 Corinthians 5:9-10)

It is not clearly stated if this judgment is about salvation or about how our service for the Lord will be evaluated before the judgment seat of Christ. One thing is clear from the teachings of the Bible; there will be a time of judgment. John said it this way in Revelation 20:12, *"And I saw the dead, small and great, standing before God, and books were opened. And another book was opened, which is the Book of Life. And the dead were judged according to their works, by the things which were written in the books."* The main point here is a question about your choice of a lifestyle. Will you live to please the Lord or to please the flesh? Will you strive to become the kind of disciple who works to produce spiritual fruit unto the Lord?

An apostle (one sent) strives to please the one who called, anointed, and sent him or her as a representative. Jesus is our role model and this is how He ministered. Look at how He says it in John 5:30, *"By myself I can do nothing; I judge only as I hear, and my judgment is just, for I seek not to please myself but him who sent me."* This is a choice each of us must make for ourselves. Paul challenges people to choose a lifestyle which will be approved by the Lord. Those who do this will be entrusted with the precious Gospel of the Kingdom. Who are you trying to please?

> *For the appeal we make does not spring from error or impure motives, nor are we trying to trick you. On the contrary, we speak as men approved by God to be entrusted with the gospel. We are not trying to please men but God, who tests our hearts.* (1 Thessalonians 2:3-4)

The things I shared in the opening paragraphs of this part of the book were not meant to offend you or to question who you are in Christ. I believe my motives were pure and free from trickery. I am simply offering you the opportunity to explore your relationship with the Lord from another perspective in hopes that it will open up a way for you to grow in the Spirit and to be elevated as a disciple of Jesus. As you look at the next three types of spiritual fruit, look at them as being primarily focused toward pleasing the Lord. Of course these fruits will also bless you and others, however I believe that the most powerful effect of allowing these three fruits of the Spirit to flow through you will be in your relationship with the Lord.

FRUIT UNTO THE LORD

> *I beseech you therefore, brethren, by the mercies of God, that you present your bodies a living sacrifice, holy, acceptable to God, which is your reasonable service. And do not be conformed to this world, but be transformed by the renewing of your mind, that you may prove what is that good and acceptable and perfect will of God.* (Romans 12:1-2)

The three fruits unto the Lord are faithfulness, goodness, and self-control. These are all primary attributes of the Lord. He has blessed us mightily through his acts of love reflected in these attributes. I remind you again that you were created in His image. As you mirror and develop these same attributes, your life and work will in a profound way be pleasing to Him. Are you becoming more and more like Him each day? If not, what should you do about it?

1. FAITHFULNESS

So God created man in His own image; in the image of God He created him; male and female He created them. Then God blessed them, and God said to them, "Be fruitful and multiply; fill the earth and subdue it; have dominion over the fish of the sea, over the birds of the air, and over every living thing that moves on the earth." (Genesis 1:27-28)

The Lord's first command to human beings was to be fruitful. This is something like a prime directive from the Lord for each person on Earth. Fruitfulness should be a primary motivation behind all that you are doing for the Kingdom. Think about it! You are blessed to be living in the midst of the great end-time harvest. The Lord chose you to live in this generation and to be a part of His great work of salvation. The fact that the Lord has placed you in this period of time speaks directly to the issue of fruitfulness. You are a worker in the harvest fields, and the Lord is looking for a good return on what He has sown. Think carefully about the next two questions. Are you doing your part to serve and please Him in your generation? Are you truly fruitful in all your acts of discipleship?

It gave me great joy to have some brothers come and tell about your faithfulness to the truth and how you continue to walk in the truth. (3 John 1:3, NIV)

I believe there is a special reason why John received so much joy through the faithfulness of his disciples. It was because he had appropriated the attributes of the Lord expressed in these fruits of the Spirit. I believe this is important for you to understand because it tells you something very significant about the Lord. He experiences joy when His children demonstrate faithfulness to Him and His Word. In other words, the fruit of faithfulness blesses the Lord. Consider what the Lord said through His prophet Isaiah:

Therefore the Lord said: "Inasmuch as these people draw near with their mouths and honor Me with their lips, but have removed their hearts far from Me, and their fear toward Me is taught by the commandment of men, therefore, behold, I will again do a marvelous work among this people, a marvelous work and a wonder; for the wisdom of their wise men shall perish, and the understanding of their prudent men shall be hidden." Woe to those who seek deep to hide their counsel far from the LORD, and their works are in the dark; they say, "Who sees us?" and, "Who knows us?" (Isaiah 29:13-15)

All the songs of praise and the beautifully phrased prayers are useless when they come through unfaithful lips. Faithfulness to the Lord unlocks the doors which in the past may have blocked or hindered your prayers and the effectiveness of your labors for the Lord. Things cannot flow in an environment of unfaithfulness. I don't mean to give you a judgment or release condemnation. I am not talking about some great sin or failure. I am actually focused on the small yet powerful things which may not always be flowing through you. The absence of these things which reflect your faithfulness is essentially unfaithfulness. It is a spiritual law. To please the Lord, faithfulness must be one of your primary attributes.

Faithfulness is the intentional process of seeking every possible way to please the Lord. I think that most believers want to do this. One of the facts about living in a body is that you will experience fatigue. At times you simply get tired and need to relax for a season. During this time, you may neglect some of the important ways of demonstrating faithfulness to the Lord. After a time of resting, it takes a great deal of energy and focus to get these attributes moving again. At this point, I have some good news. You don't have to do it. The Holy Spirit will do it if you ask. You didn't produce these attributes in your life. They came as gifts from the Spirit, and He can reactivate and reenergize them. Ask and you will receive.

To help you understand this concept, think of it in terms of what pleases you. Parents grieve when their children are unfaithful. Children basically desire to please their parents, but it takes concentration and effort. From time to time they get lax in the things which please their parents. They don't do it intentionally. It just happens during a time of neglect. It is the same with the Lord. God is our good Father and He is grieved by any lack of faithfulness. He is longsuffering which many people mistake for approval. Like our children, we can just forget for a time the positive things which please Him. This lesson is a reminder to get them flowing again. It is better to see it and respond now than to wait for a time of judgment. The truth is that a day of reckoning is coming. Are the Lord's people ready for it?

When the spiritual fruit of faithfulness is flowing in our lives, we will not grieve the Holy Spirit. This is so important, because He is the source of this fruit in our lives and ministry. In fact, all of these fruits are supernatural. All of them are gifts from the Holy Spirit and are not natural in fallen humanity. It is our nature to seek for self and rebel against authority. Only with the Lord's help can we possibly produce this fruit. Spiritual fruits don't flow because we have trained ourselves or lifted ourselves up by our own boot straps. They flow in us and through us because we are willing to allow Him to work in our lives.

When fruitfulness manifests in our lives, the Lord is pleased and sends abundant blessings. Leviticus 26:9, *"For I will look on you favorably and make you fruitful, multiply you and confirm My covenant with you."* The Lord is so amazing and wonderful. He gives the gifts of the Spirit. Then He gives you the power and authority to use them. Basically, He does all the work and then rewards you for letting it happen. It doesn't get any better than this. This too is somewhat like our relationship with our own children. We give them money, take them shopping for a gift to give us, help them buy it, and then wrap it for them. When they hand the gift to us, we are excited and praise the child for doing something wonderful. This is how Father God works with us. Amen?

I don't know about you, but I am being filled with joy just thinking about the spiritual fruits the Lord is working through you and me. If you get some assistance from these lessons and demonstrate your faithfulness to the Lord I will be filled with joy just as John was. I believe it is going to happen. So, I am filled with gratitude right now and I want to give Him genuine and pure worship, praise, honor and glory. Amen? Now, think about this one last thing. If this fruit is missing in your life, can you truthfully say you are in the will of God?

2. GOODNESS

Therefore we also pray always for you that our God would count you worthy of this calling, and fulfill all the good pleasure of His goodness and the work of faith with power, that the name of our

*Lord Jesus Christ may be glorified in you, and you
in Him, according to the grace of our God and
the Lord Jesus Christ.* (2 Thessalonians 1:11-12)

Paul makes it clear that the Lord is very pleased with the
fruit of goodness. Isn't that an amazing thought? The goodness
comes from Him and it still gives Him good pleasure to see it
working in and through you and me. Again, it seems like something that happens with human parents. I believe this is how
the Lord helps us to understand how this works. We work hard
on our child's project for school and then cover him/her with
praise when it succeeds. What a beautiful image this gives of
our Father God.

Sometimes I can imagine Him looking at you and joyfully
proclaiming, "That's my boy!" or "That's my girl!" Then He
exclaims, "Look at their goodness!" Imagine the pride in his
workmanship. Remember what He said to Moses when He was
asked to show His glory. He said, I will show you my goodness. Goodness is a kind of summary of all the attributes of the
Lord. When you give Him the spiritual fruit of goodness, you
are demonstrating how all these fruits are manifesting in your
life. In the passage below notice very carefully what the Lord
is saying through the prophet Jeremiah. The Lord receives great
joy in doing good things for you and me.

*"Then it shall be to Me a name of joy, a praise,
and an honor before all nations of the earth, who
shall hear all the good that I do to them; they shall
fear and tremble for all the goodness and all the
prosperity that I provide for it."* (Jeremiah 33:9)

There is great power in the goodness of the Lord. The spiritual fruit of goodness has an impact on all the nations of the
earth. Every nation which sees the goodness of the Lord will
be inspired to give Him praise and honor. I believe this speaks

of how rare real Biblical goodness is in our generation. When it manifests, the world will take note of it. When you display His goodness, you release that power into those around you. The ultimate outcome of the fruit of goodness is to release praise and honor to the Lord. This is your calling and it is wonderful in His sight. Amen?

When we live in God's will and accomplish His purposes and plans for our lives, we make Him a proud Papa. Isn't that a wonderful thought? The things that produce good in our lives bring pride and joy to Him. The Lord's purpose in giving the fruit of goodness is summed up by Solomon in Proverbs 2:20-21, *"So you may walk in the way of goodness, and keep to the paths of righteousness. For the upright will dwell in the land, and the blameless will remain in it;"* As you flow with the spiritual fruit of goodness, you are keeping yourself on the righteous paths of the Lord. Now ask yourself this question. If the fruit of goodness is missing in your life, can you really claim to be in the will of God?

3. SELF-CONTROL

But know this, that in the last days perilous times will come: For men will be lovers of themselves, lovers of money, boasters, proud, blasphemers, disobedient to parents, unthankful, unholy, unloving, unforgiving, slanderers, without self-control, brutal, despisers of good, traitors, headstrong, haughty, lovers of pleasure rather than lovers of God, having a form of godliness but denying its power. And from such people turn away! (2 Timothy 3:1-5)

Paul tells Timothy that a lack of self-control will characterize many people in the last days. I am sometimes convinced that we must be living in the last days, because the conditions referenced in this passage of scripture seem to be very common in our generation. It is time to drop the empty forms of godliness which deny the power of God to work in the body of Christ. It is time to get back to the basics of our faith. One of those basics is to see and understand that one of the primary fruits of the Spirit is self-control. How are you doing with self-control? Once again, I remind you that it is important for you to evaluate yourself in these things rather than focusing on the limitations or failures you see in others.

In our generation, we see many people who proudly claim to have no control over their impulses. The lack of impulse control has actually become an official form of diagnosing character defects. I know the term "character defect" is not politically correct, however it is the truth. We tend to excuse the bad behavior of people we diagnosis as mentally or emotionally challenged. This kind of diagnosis is often used in courtrooms in an attempt to excuse some very terrible behaviors. Our government and our criminal justice system have certainly gone the way of people described by Paul in his letter to Timothy.

You may not be able to do very much about these huge political systems, but you can do something about your part in them. You will be held accountable for failing to exercise self-control. There are no excuses which can nullify what the Lord has decreed and how He says He will judge. I like how The Message Bible translated Proverbs 25:28, "*A person without self-control is like a house with its doors and windows knocked out.*" How are your spiritual doors and windows? If they have been knocked out, you are not living in a very secure place.

A good example of making the wrong choice about self-control is seen in the life of Felix the Roman Governor. You can read this in Acts 24:25, "*Now as he reasoned about righteousness, self-control, and the judgment to come, Felix was afraid and answered, 'Go away for now; when I have a convenient time I will call for you.'*" Felix was wise enough to be fearful of the judgment to come. When he heard about the issues of righteousness and self-control fear motivated him to try to delay the time when he needed to make a decision for himself. He wanted to wait for a more convenient time. As far as we know that time never came. You cannot escape judgment by ignoring it. There is no time which is more convenient than right now. Be certain that you don't make the mistake of Felix.

The self-control exercised by a true disciple keeps God first and self in service. Listen to what Solomon had to say about it in Proverbs 14:29, *"He who is slow to wrath has great understanding, but he who is impulsive exalts folly."* I don't recommend a plea of lacking impulse control when you approach the Lord. Embracing a lifestyle of folly which serves the flesh alone will always put you in opposition to God. It is far better to accept Peter's advice in the passage below.

> *But also for this very reason, giving all diligence, add to your faith virtue, to virtue knowledge, to knowledge self-control, to self-control perseverance, to perseverance godliness, to godliness brotherly kindness, and to brotherly kindness love. For if these things are yours and abound, you will be neither barren nor unfruitful in the knowledge of our Lord Jesus Christ. For he who lacks these things is shortsighted, even to blindness, and has forgotten that he was cleansed from his old sins.* (2 Peter 1:5-9)

A lack of self-control tends to elevate self above God. This should never happen in the lives of the followers of Yeshua ha Messiach. We must not exhibit the problem present in the church at Ephesus. Revelation 2:4-5, *"Nevertheless I have this against you, that you have left your first love. Remember therefore from where you have fallen; repent and do the first works, or else I will come to you quickly and remove your lampstand from its place—unless you repent."* What can a church do without its lampstand (Holy Spirit)? If the Holy Spirit is grieved and departs from you, all of your spiritual gifts and all of the fruit of the Spirit go with Him. This must not happen in the Church of Jesus Christ or in the lives of His true followers.

The Lord is offering us another opportunity to repent and get right with Him. This is the true meaning of righteousness. It is being in a right relationship with the Lord. Self-control is a key element of this relationship. It is a spiritual fruit that we minister unto the Lord. It must be present if we plan to please Him. Once again, ask yourself the question: If this fruit is missing from your life and ministry, are you really in the will of God?

> *Now the word of the LORD came to me, saying: "Son of man, you dwell in the midst of a rebellious house, which has eyes to see but does not see, and ears to hear but does not hear; for they are a rebellious house."* (Ezekiel 12:12)

Ask the Lord to release a greater seer anointing to you so that you can shine the light of His truth into every blind spot in your character. If you do not see what the Lord is revealing to you, it may be a rebellious spirit manifesting through you. You need to purge every remnant of a rebellious spirit if you want to please the Lord. Ask the Holy Spirit to help you see if there is any character defect lurking in the dark area of your soul? Is there a lack of self-control in your life which you have been failing to see? You need eyes to see and ears to hear what the Lord is saying to you in these last days.

During their forty plus years of wandering around in the wilderness, the children of Israel were still spiritually blind. They had seen the Lord's miracles, signs and wonders. With their own eyes they had seen the sea part as they walked across on dry land. They had seen the pillar of cloud by day and the column of fire by night. With their own eyes they had seen the ten wonders the Lord had worked to free them from bondage in Egypt.

They had eaten manna. After crying out for meat, they saw birds come to them and pile up knee deep. They had seen all of these, but failed to understand their relationship with the Lord.

Study the passage below and consider your relationship with the Lord. You may be in a church or ministry where healings, miracles, signs and wonders regularly manifest. After seeing all these things, have you failed to understand what the Lord is doing for His people? Have these signs and wonders failed to awaken your seer anointing? Have you failed to manifest the spiritual fruits unto the Lord mentioned in this study? If so, I have some good news for you. You still have time to make a fresh start with the Lord. Today is the perfect day to let the Holy Spirit lead you back into a right relationship with the Lord. Amen?

> *Now Moses called all Israel and said to them: "You have seen all that the Lord did before your eyes in the land of Egypt, to Pharaoh and to all his servants and to all his land—the great trials which your eyes have seen, the signs, and those great wonders. Yet the LORD has not given you a heart to perceive and eyes to see and ears to hear, to this very day. And I have led you forty years in the wilderness. Your clothes have not worn out on you, and your sandals have not worn out on your feet. You have not eaten bread, nor have you drunk wine or similar drink, that you may know that I am the LORD your God.* (Deuteronomy 19:2-6)

PRAYERS

> *And this I pray, that your love may abound still more and more in knowledge and all discernment, that you may approve the things that are excellent, that you may be sincere and without offense*

till the day of Christ, being filled with the fruits of righteousness which are by Jesus Christ, to the glory and praise of God." (Philippians 1:9-11)

*For this reason we also, since the day we heard it, do not cease to pray for you, and to ask that you may be filled with the knowledge of His will in all wisdom and spiritual understanding; that you may walk worthy of the Lord, fully pleasing Him, being **fruitful in every good work** and increasing in the knowledge of God; strengthened with all might, according to His glorious power, for all patience and longsuffering with joy; giving thanks to the Father who has qualified us to be partakers of the inheritance of the saints in the light. He has delivered us from the power of darkness and conveyed us into the kingdom of the Son of His love, in whom we have redemption through His blood, the forgiveness of sins.* (Colossians 1:9-14)

PART THREE

DESTINIES REVEALED IN SPIRITUAL GIFTS

Even so you, since you are zealous for spiritual gifts, let it be for the edification of the church that you seek to excel. (I Corinthians 14:12)

In the twelfth chapter of First Corinthians, Paul lists nine gifts of the Spirit. As with the nine fruits of the Spirit, these gifts can be subdivided into three groups of three. The three groups are; gifts of revelation, gifts of power and gifts of speech. In the next four chapters we will go through a detailed study of each of these gifts. There are several important reasons for this study. First, your identity is partially revealed by the gifts you receive from the Holy Spirit. As you get clarity about who you are in Christ through these gifts, it becomes very important for you to better understand your gifts to maximize their use in your life. The final reason for this study is to help you activate these spiritual gifts in your life and ministry.

A key concept for this study is: Remember you are who the Lord gifted you to be. That is good news. Now listen to some better news. He hasn't stopped releasing more and more potential into your life through the gifts of the Holy Spirit. Some people teach that each person is blessed to receive only one gift. This teaching is based on the notion that the Holy Spirit limits the gifts available to each person so that we will all understand that we need each other. According to this theory, we are only complete when we join our gifts together. There is some truth in this, but it isn't the whole truth. We do need to come together as the body of Christ, and He has chosen to build us up this way. However, nothing in the Word says that you can only have one gift.

Listen to Paul's teaching in 1 Corinthians 14:1, *"Pursue love, and desire spiritual gifts, but especially that you may prophesy."* Paul would not have deceived us this way if we were only authorized one gift. If you have a spiritual gift, that is wonderful, but you don't have to settle for just one. Think about what Paul is decreeing in 1 Corinthians 1:7, *"Therefore you do not lack any spiritual gift as you eagerly wait for our Lord Jesus Christ to be revealed."* Think about this. You are not meant to be lacking in any of the spiritual gifts. The Lord will give you every gift you need to accomplish your mission for the Kingdom of God. It is appropriate for you to seek all the other spiritual gifts as long as you first pursue love. It is important to remember that the Lord can only gift you with what your love can carry. As your love for others grows, more gifts will be released to you. Begin now to pursue the love of God and watch all the amazing things He will begin to release to you and through you.

> *Therefore we also pray always for you that our God would count you worthy of this calling, and fulfill all the good pleasure of His goodness and the work of faith with power, that the name of our Lord Jesus Christ may be glorified in you, and you in Him, according to the grace of our God and the Lord Jesus Christ.* (2 Thessalonians 1:11-12)

Chapter Seven

REVEALED IN YOUR GIFTS OF REVELATION

In an early morning vision, I was lifted up in the Spirit to a position just outside the massive wall and gates of the Kingdom of Heaven. As I looked at this almost impenetrable barrier, I sought a way to enter. The Lord made it clear that people still enter the same old way. He said, "Enter the gates with thanksgiving!" That is it. It is not about our wisdom, worthiness, titles or accomplishments. It is all about Him. We can only enter wearing His robe of righteousness and the garment of praise which He gives. I went back to Psalm 100:4-5, *"Enter into His gates with thanksgiving, and into His courts with praise. Be thankful to Him, and bless His name. For the Lord is good; His mercy is everlasting, and His truth endures to all generations."*

I am ready to enter. How about you? Today is a good day to visit the Lord in Heaven. I started the same old way this morning. Psalm 100:1-3, *"Make a joyful shout to the Lord, all you lands! Serve the Lord with gladness; Come before His presence with singing. Know that the Lord, He is God; It is He who has made us, and not we ourselves; we are His people and the sheep of His pasture."* There is no mystery here except why we don't go to Him more often.

After I entered the gates, the Lord showed me something which surprised me. I saw people with powerful spiritual gifts kneeling before people who needed impartation. They were putting what they had received into the hands of those in need. Did you catch that? Those in need were standing and those with the gifts were kneeling. In our human way, we tend to think that those in need ought to be kneeling. However, those with the real power gifts of the Spirit have no problem kneeling in order to release something to another person. Then I heard the Lord say, "If you have received a spiritual gift, you need to be imparting it to others! I want the Gospel of the Kingdom to spread by contact like an infectious disease!" Okay! That surprised me too. No mystery here! We enter the gates to receive the gifts and then spread them by contact. Are you ready for this? Now is the time to humbly submit to the Lord and obediently spread the gifts of the Spirit to as many others as possible.

Then the Lord said, "I am releasing unmerited grace today! Don't try to qualify people! Great grace is being released today! Impart as much of it as you can!" My thoughts went to Ephesians 4:29, "*Let no corrupt word proceed out of your mouth, but what is good for necessary edification, that it may impart grace to the hearers.*" There is a strong anointing today to impart grace. Notice that Paul is teaching that we need to adjust what is coming out of our mouths in order to impart grace. Speak what is good today and every day so that you may impart grace to those who are listening to you.

Today enter the gates to receive and impart gifts and release great grace to as many people as possible! Sounds simple doesn't it. So, why isn't more of it happening? By now this great grace should have been imparted to the whole world. I believe a key to understanding this is given by Paul in Ephesians 4:30-32, "*And do not grieve the Holy Spirit of God, by whom you were sealed for the day of redemption. Let all bitterness, wrath, anger, clamor, and evil speaking be put away from you, with all malice. And be kind to one another, tenderhearted, forgiving one another, even as God in Christ forgave you."* Did you catch it? Many people need an attitude adjustment in order to impart the grace being released by the Lord.

I pray that the Lord will do a mighty work today in renewing our minds and transforming our souls so that we can receive and impart the gifts of the Spirit and the grace of God! I pray that we will let go of everything which hinders and step out in faith to spread the good news of the gospel of the Kingdom to as many people as possible! May it spread more and more and further and further until the Lord returns and finds us faithfully doing His work! Amen and Amen!!!

REVIEW

Before getting into the heart of this teaching, I want to give you a quick review of what we have covered so far. We started this study with the statement: God has a plan for your life. It is a good plan. The Lord does not want to harm you! It is very important to know that the Lord wants good things for you. It is a plan to prosper you and to give you hope and a future. This message given through the prophet Jeremiah is also consistent with the teachings of the New Testament. Consider what James wrote about the gifts coming from the Lord.

> *Do not be deceived, my beloved brethren. Every good gift and every perfect gift is from above, and comes down from the Father of lights, with whom there is no variation or shadow of turning. Of His own will He brought us forth by the word of truth, that we might be a kind of firstfruits of His creatures.* (James 1:16-17)

Then we looked at ways you can determine if you're in God's will. You can prove it by the presence of the fruit of the Spirit working in and through you. You will also get a clear

149

picture of who you are in Christ when you see what you will look like when all these spiritual fruits are flowing through you. In the book of Galatians, Paul lists nine fruits of the spirit. There are three categories of the fruit of the Spirit. First: is the fruit for your own life: love, joy, and peace. Next: Fruit into the lives of others: longsuffering, kindness, and gentleness. And finally, Fruit unto God: faithfulness, goodness, and self-control. Why does the Lord want you to bear so much fruit? Jesus made it clear in His teachings about bearing fruit.

> *When you bear (produce) much fruit, My Father is honored and glorified, and you show and prove yourselves to be true followers of Mine."* (John 15:8, Amplified)

NINE GIFTS OF THE SPIRIT

> *There are diversities of gifts, but the same Spirit. There are differences of ministries, but the same Lord. And there are diversities of activities, but it is the same God who works all in all. But the manifestation of the Spirit is given to each one for the profit of all: for to one is given the word of wisdom through the Spirit, to another the word of knowledge through the same Spirit, to another faith by the same Spirit, to another gifts of healings by the same Spirit, to another the working of miracles, to another prophecy, to another discerning of spirits, to another different kinds of tongues, to another the interpretation of tongues. But one and the same Spirit works all these things, distributing to each one individually as He wills.* (1 Corinthians 12:4-11)

In the passage above, Paul lists nine gifts of the Spirit. In this teaching, Paul says that each gift is given in accordance with the will of the Spirit. In other words, spiritual gifts are tailor-made for the individuals who are receiving them. They do not come by accident. They are given in accordance with the will of God to accomplish specific purposes in the establishment of His Kingdom. When you receive spiritual gifts it is not a coincident. It is not by the will of man. It is by the will of God. He gives them to you in order to help you accomplish your destiny. These gifts demonstrate a major part of your identity in Jesus Christ. They tell the world who you are. They also reveal this to you. They reveal who you are in Christ and what your destiny is for the Kingdom of God.

These nine spiritual gifts break down into three groups of three similar to the groupings of the fruits of the Spirit. The prophetic significance of the number three is completeness. The number three points specifically to the nature of God. God manifests Himself as Father, Son and Holy Spirit. In each area of His creation, the number three represents divine completeness. It is the formula for order in all created things. For example, you were created with a spirit, a soul and a body. All other created matter can be categorized as either animal, vegetable or mineral. The cosmos consist of the Heavens, Earth and Hell.

The prophetic significance of the number nine takes this even further. Nine consists of three times three. It can literally be understood as completeness multiplied by completeness. So, you can see that the number nine can be understood to represent the divine completeness of all things. You can clearly see this concept of completeness in the nine fruits of the Spirit. It is not a coincidence that spiritual gifts come in a set of nine. When the Lord decided to provide the nine spiritual gifts, it was to give the completeness of all that is needed for the body of Christ to accomplish its purpose.

When you look at spiritual gifts, it is always appropriate to think about purpose. There are no accidents in the work of the Lord. Each of these gifts individually have purpose and the totality of the gifts provides completeness of purpose. It is important to understand that these gifts are given for the edification of the church. Remember what Paul wrote in 1 Corinthians 14:12, *"Even so you, since you are zealous for spiritual gifts, let it be for the edification of the church that you seek to excel."* All of the gifts have the purpose of building up the Church of Jesus Christ. You can know you're in God's will when spiritual gifts are present and active. To see the will of God active in the gifts, make a careful study of the passage below.

> *And it shall come to pass afterward that I will (God's will) pour out My Spirit on all flesh; your sons and your daughters shall prophesy, your old men shall dream dreams, your young men shall see visions. And also on My menservants and on My maidservants I will pour out My Spirit in those days.* (Joel 2:28-29)

Since that first outpouring of the Holy Spirit, fire and power on the Day of Pentecost, we've been living in the days the Lord spoke of through the prophet Joel. The Lord made it clear in this prophecy that spiritual gifts are for all of the Lord's people and not just for those living in that time or in that locality. The Lord clearly states that He will pour out His spirit, His gifts and His power on all flesh. You can put your full trust in this truth: Spiritual gifts are intended for every believer. They are available to young and old, rich and poor, male and female. This is completeness. Nothing is lacking in the gifts of the Lord.

I believe that it is un-natural for any believer to lack a desire for spiritual gifts. The Bible directs us to desire spiritual gifts. Remember 1 Corinthians 14:1, *"Pursue love, and desire spiritual gifts..."* Notice again the order of these things. To become all the Lord created you to be, you must first pursue love and then seek spiritual gifts. As you seek spiritual gifts, there are two very important things to remember. First, you should seek the gifts which build up and strengthen the church. After this, seek the spiritual gifts which will help you to accomplish God's will in your life. In the passage below, notice that Paul is saying it gives the Lord pleasure to work His will in and through you.

> *Therefore, my beloved, as you have always obeyed,*
> *not as in my presence only, but now much more*
> *in my absence, work out your own salvation with*
> *fear and trembling; for it is God who works in*
> *you both to will and to do for His good pleasure.*
> (Philippians 2:12-13)

THE FIRST SET OF SPIRITUAL GIFTS
THREE GIFTS OF REVELATION

There are three spiritual gifts which can best be understood as gifts of revelation knowledge. All of these gifts have a central focus. They are spiritual gifts which assist you in being led by the Holy Spirit. Think about what Paul was saying in Romans 8:14, "*For as many as are led by the Spirit of God, these are sons of God.*" Can we really claim to be sons and daughters of God if we are not led by the Holy Spirit? I don't think so. How about you? What do you think?

The church in its entirety has not done well at teaching in this area. Many churches believe the release of spiritual gifts was a phenomena which ended with the first apostles. Clearly this was not Paul's intent in his message to the church in Rome. None of them were a part of that original group. This is clearly a teaching for all believers for all time. It is tragic that many believers have accepted this false teaching and live in denial of the availability of these gifts for present day disciples of Yeshua ha Messiach. May that never be said of you or me! Amen?

REVELATION GIFT ONE
THE WORD OF WISDOM

...for to one is given the word of wisdom through the Spirit... (1 Corinthians 12:8)

As we unpack this teaching for better understanding, take note that in this passage it was the Greek word "logos" which was translated as "word." "Logos" is normally understood as the spoken word. This gift involves someone speaking and another person hearing. It is the Holy Spirit who is speaking and you and I should be listening to His words. It is time to get your spiritual ears opened wide so that you can hear the voice of the Lord speaking to and through you. Once again, earnestly seek to activate and increase your seer anointing to help you maximize what the Lord is offering to you.

As you embrace this gift, remember that you may hear a word being spoken into your spirit. On the other hand you may see a word as in a vision. In addition, it is possible that you will see an image which represents the word being given. It is also possible that you will feel the message being given. People who operate in a feeler anointing often experience various feeling as words of wisdom. Those who are gifted to minister in this way often experience the pain of another person as they minister. It is not their pain. It is a revelation about the pain another person is feeling. Don't be surprised if you feel certain physical and spiritual issues or pain while ministering under the leadership of the Holy Spirit.

The word "wisdom" in this passage comes from the Greek word "*sophia.*" This word points to the correct application of knowledge. The word of wisdom may come to you after you receive a word of knowledge. The word of wisdom tells you what to do with a word of knowledge. It may also tell you when, where and how you are to apply a word of knowledge. The word of wisdom is more than just knowing something. It's knowing how to use that information for a purpose. It is not about your purpose, but the Lord's purpose being worked out through you.

The Word of God clearly delineates at least three distinct types of wisdom. When we speak of wisdom in this context, it is important to be clear about which specific type of wisdom is being considered. The three types are: the wisdom of God, the wisdom of the world and the wisdom of man. There is a significant difference between each of these types of wisdom. If you are going to minister effectively, you must know which kind of wisdom you are receiving. Many times when people are confused about this, they minister their own wisdom or the wisdom of the world and represent it to others as the wisdom of God. We must avoid this kind of mistake.

1. THE WISDOM OF GOD

However, we speak wisdom among those who are mature, yet not the wisdom of this age, nor of the rulers of this age, who are coming to nothing. But we speak the wisdom of God in a mystery, the hidden wisdom which God ordained before the ages for our glory, which none of the rulers of this age knew; for had they known, they would not have crucified the Lord of glory. (1 Corinthians 2:6-8)

As we consider this first type of wisdom, it is important to know the meaning of the word mystery in the New Testament. Basically, the word mystery describes something which was formerly hidden, but now has been revealed to us. Father God has made all these mysteries known in the revelation of Yeshua ha Messiach and through the work of the Holy Spirit. Remember how Jesus promised in John 16:13, *"However, when He, the Spirit of truth, has come, He will guide you into all truth; for He will not speak on His own authority, but whatever He hears He will speak; and He will tell you things to come."* Father God has made these mysteries known so that you can more effectively proclaim the Gospel of the Kingdom. The wisdom of God will always demonstrate the attributes of the Lord. Consider how this is described in the passage below.

> *But the wisdom that is from above is first pure, then peaceable, gentle, willing to yield, full of mercy and good fruits, without partiality and without hypocrisy."* (James 3:17)

The question emerges: How do you recognize God's wisdom? I always like to say at this point: I'm glad you asked. The Lord has given us a kind of litmus test so that we can verify that our revelations are truly from Him. This has been revealed to us so that we can be certain that our understanding is correct and is based on His truth. When the revelation comes, you can apply the characteristics of God given truth revealed in the passage from James. You can ask if it is pure, peaceable and gentle. Does it yield the fruit of the Spirit? Is it filled with mercy? Is it without partiality and hypocrisy? Neither the wisdom of the world nor the wisdom of man can pass this test.

2. THE WISDOM OF THE WORLD

> *However, we speak wisdom among those who are mature, yet not the wisdom of this age, nor of the rulers of this age, who are coming to nothing."* (1 Corinthians 2:6)

One of Paul's key concepts about the wisdom of the world is that it is *"coming to nothing."* When I first read this, I thought about all the nutritional pronouncements from so called science during the past generation which have now been soundly debunked. It seems that the scientific concepts embraced almost universally today will be in the category of junk science tomorrow. This can be troubling for people as they strive to choose whom they can trust. Paul's answer is that the wisdom of this world is coming to nothing. Don't make the mistake of founding your life or ministry on the wisdom of the world. The tragic consequences of much of our worldly wisdom is that people sincerely striving to know the truth are being misled and they may eventually be left hopeless.

But if you have bitter envy and self-seeking in your hearts, do not boast and lie against the truth. This wisdom does not descend from above, but is earthly, sensual, demonic. (James 3:14-15)

In the realm of religious knowledge, how do you recognize worldly wisdom as opposed to the wisdom of the Lord? The writer of the book of James gives us another test we can apply in this area. Consider the outcomes of applying a word of wisdom. Does it lead to bitter envy? Does it come from impure motives such as self-seeking? Does it boast or lie about the wisdom of God? If it contains any or all of these qualities, you can know that it comes from the wisdom of the world. You need to avoid all these forms of worldly wisdom. This will not be easy since you live in the world and have to function as a member of your community or nation. The good news is that you are not left without resources. The Holy Spirit has been sent to guide you. You should always seek wisdom from Him before making a major decision.

3. THE WISDOM OF MAN

The wisdom of man refers to information solely based on your own ability to think and to reason. This is your own wisdom. People who consider themselves wise by the standards of this world tend to fall into error. This kind of thinking usually leads to pride and pride goes before a fall. Remember Solomon's sound advice given in Proverbs 16:18, *"Pride goes before destruction, and a haughty spirit before a fall."* He knew this from personal experience. Listen to his confession from the book of Ecclesiastes.

> *I communed with my heart, saying, "Look, I have attained greatness, and have gained more wisdom than all who were before me in Jerusalem. My heart has understood great wisdom and knowledge.* (Ecclesiastes 1:16)

On the surface this may sound good, but we know the rest of the story. All these thoughts preceded his fall from the grace of God. After being given all this wisdom and understanding by the Lord, he still made the most basic forms of bad decisions. In his later years, he even turned to idolatry under the influence of his foreign wives. Think about it. After attaining all the worldly symbols of success, Solomon stated over and over that everything in his life was empty. It all came to nothing, because his pride led him into error and eventually resulted in a great fall.

THE GIFT OF WORDS OF WISDOM

The gift of the "word of wisdom" is based on the first type of wisdom. It is the wisdom of God. It is the supernatural impartation of facts and understanding. It is not natural. It does not proceed from the wisdom of the world or the wisdom of man. It comes as a pure gift of the Lord delivered by the Holy Spirit. It may not make sense by worldly standards, because it is far superior to the natural order of things. You can only use this wisdom effectively by operating in faith. Trust what the Lord is telling you as you step out in obedience to do the work of the Kingdom.

*Therefore settle it in your hearts not to medi-
tate beforehand on what you will answer; for
I will give you a mouth and wisdom which all
your adversaries will not be able to contradict or
resist.* (Luke 21:14-15)

When a word of wisdom is given, you are enabled to express
the Holy Spirit's revelation knowledge in a particular situation.
You will be enabled to give answers to a person, group or church
based on the wisdom of God. This does not come from any
natural ability you possess. We are talking about a completely
different kind of gift. It is a revelation coming directly from the
Holy Spirit. In that moment, He gives you the ability to apply
wisdom and understanding which comes as a pure gift from
above. Remember James 1:17, *"Every good gift and every perfect gift is from above, and comes down from the Father of lights,
with whom there is no variation or shadow of turning."* When
we talk about this spiritual gift or capability, we are speaking
of the ability to deliver prophecy, knowledge, faith, healing or
other gifts from the Lord in such a way that it will bring about
the greatest possible success.

When these gifts manifest, you will know that you are in
God's will. Be aware: none of the spiritual gifts are given to
disobedient and rebellious people. It is important to understand
that to live in God's will in the world today you need the revelation gifts. You need to say the right words at the right time
in the right way in order to lead people to Christ. Being able to
do this effectively is a gift from God. It is not about your natural abilities. It is about something supernatural coming directly
from the Lord. If you don't feel adequate to do these things, that
is good news, because you are not capable of these things. They
are supernatural and the Lord is giving them to you and through
you to others. If you don't feel up to the task then go to the Holy
Spirit! Ask for the wisdom to follow Jesus. Trust what the Word
of God says about the way to gain wisdom.

If any of you lacks wisdom, let him ask of God,
who gives to all liberally and without reproach,
and it will be given to him. (James 1:5)

REVELATION GIFT TWO THE WORD
OF KNOWLEDGE

...to another the word of knowledge through the
same Spirit... (1 Corinthians 12:8)

The word "knowledge" used in this passage comes from
the Greek word "*gnosis*." The root meaning of this word is to
understanding a thing. In other words, the Holy Spirit is giving
you a supernatural understanding of situations, problems, and
or facts. This kind of knowledge does not come by any human
means. It is God given! The Holy Spirit is your only source for
this precious and powerful gift.

In reality, this is revelation knowledge about the divine plan
and will of God for a person, group or nation. It is knowledge
received directly from the Holy Spirit. It is how you know what
to say or do in a difficult situation. This gift is one of the primary ways the Holy Spirit leads you to accomplish your purpose in the Kingdom of God. This is one of the powerful ways
the Holy Spirit reveals who you are in Christ. Remember that
wisdom and knowledge always work together. Solomon says in
Proverbs 1:7, "*The fear of the Lord is the beginning of knowl-*
edge" You cannot operate in this gift unless you have a deep and
abiding sense of awe for the Lord and all His words and works.

Remember that these words of knowledge are all gifts of
the Holy Spirit. They are Holy Spirit inspired, God given gifts
for your ministry in the Kingdom of God. This is how The
Lord works through the Holy Spirit to teach His disciples how
to do the right things in season. A word of knowledge brings
the reality of the Living Christ to the exact point of need in

someone's life and work. It can be best understood as knowledge from the Holy Spirit for effective ministry.

> *For this is good and acceptable in the sight of God our Savior, who desires all men to be saved and to come to the knowledge of the truth.*
> (1 Timothy 2:3-4)

When the gift of revelation knowledge is present and working, you will know that you are in God's will. This kind of knowledge does not come through any human means. This knowledge is always a gift of God for the people of God. Remember that this is one of the primary ways the Holy Spirit leads you. I want to remind you again of what Paul said in Romans 8:14, *"For as many as are led by the Spirit of God, these are sons of God."* When you are led by the Spirit of God you have the assurance that you are His and He is working through you.

REVELATION GIFT THREE
THE DISCERNING OF SPIRITS

> *...to another discerning of spirits...*
> (1 Corinthians 12:10)

The word "discerning" used in this passage comes from the Greek word *"diakrisis."* It literally means a distinguishing or a clear discrimination between two or more things. In this case, it refers to discerning between various kinds of spirits. It is referring to a Holy Spirit gift which provides you with the ability to judge by evidence whether spirits or other things are evil or of God. By this gift you can know if things are clean or unclean; holy or unholy. You will know if they are from God rather than another kind of spirit. This gift is critically important for those living in this generation.

161

*And this I pray, that your love may abound still
more and more in knowledge and all discernment,
that you may approve the things that are excellent,
that you may be sincere and without offense till
the day of Christ,* (Philippians 1:9-10)

The gift of discerning of spirits is the supernatural ability to determine the source of spiritual manifestations and to determine if they are from God. You have to be very careful with this gift. It has been misused so many times in church history. Many people have claimed to have this gift as they work to judge and or condemn other people. This is not the purpose of the gift. This behavior is one of the best ways to know that a person is operating from the wisdom of the world rather than the wisdom of God.

As with all spiritual gifts, you need to exercise this gift in order to keep it and to grow with it. This gift can be understood as operating something like a muscle. If you do not use it, it will tend to atrophy. The more you exercise the gift the stronger it becomes. This is why it is so unwise to be lax in the use of the spiritual gifts which have been given to you. They are given for a purpose and will only remain strong as long as you are focused on your God-given mission. The writer of Hebrews specifically points to this gift in the passage below. Special attention is given to the gift of discerning of spirits because deception seems to weaken this area first.

*But solid food belongs to those who are of full
age, that is, those who by reason of use have their
senses exercised to discern both good and evil.*
(Hebrews 5:14)

Discerning of spirits is a specific and definite gift of the Holy Spirit. It is the means the Lord has chosen to let you know the plans and activities of the enemy. This is also God's means of protecting you from deception. By it, God protects you in spirit, soul and body. By it the Lord helps you to preserve the purity of your Christian walk. Think about what Solomon was trying to say in Proverbs 15:21, *"Folly is joy to him who is destitute of discernment, but a man of understanding walks uprightly."* Whatever else may come against you and your ministry, I pray that you will never be destitute of discernment. Amen?

I want you to be certain that you can trust the Lord in this area. You can be certain that the Holy Spirit will bear witness with your spirit if things are of God. With this gift you are enabled to know which things are of God; which things are of the devil, and which things come from the wisdom of man. This gift does not involve any type of mind reading or any psychic power. It is the Holy Spirit at work in and through you. All believers should seek and exercise this gift. By these gifts you will know that you are in God's will. This gift will help you understand who you are in Jesus Christ. Claim the promise given to you in the passage below. Read it aloud and decree that it will manifest in your life and ministry.

> *Yes, if you cry out for discernment, and lift up your voice for understanding, if you seek her as silver, and search for her as for hidden treasures; then you will understand the fear of the LORD, and find the knowledge of God.* (Proverbs 2:3-5)

SCRIPTURE TELLS US TO EMBRACE AND CELEBRATE THESE GIFTS

God imparts spiritual understanding to you through these gifts of revelation knowledge. These are the "keys" to unlock your spirit and activate your love. If the gifts are not present, you need to turn to God for help. If you are not flowing in these gifts, you may need to examine your heart and get right with

God. To prepare you to receive the wonderful gifts prophesied in the book of Joel, take note of how God admonishes you in the following passage.

> *Now, therefore, says the* Lord, *Turn to Me with all your heart, with fasting, with weeping, and with mourning." So rend your heart, and not your garments; return to the Lord your God, for He is gracious and merciful, slow to anger, and of great kindness; and He relents from doing harm.*
> (Joel 2:12-13)

Through these spiritual gifts, you are enabled to better express your love and admiration to God. Through these gifts you are able to minister to a hungry, lost and dying world. Through the proper use of these gifts, you are being obedient to the leading of our Lord. You must not neglect them or run from them. You are called to embrace them and use them under the guidance and supervision of the Holy Spirit. Perhaps it is time to "rend your heart." If you have strayed from your gifting, it is not too late. The Lord is calling once again for His people to *"return to the Lord your God."* You can be certain that *"He is gracious and merciful, slow to anger, and of great kindness; and He relents from doing harm."* Amen? If you need to do this, don't delay. Do it right now and let the Holy Spirit reactivate and strengthen your gifting.

There is only one source for these spiritual gifts. Don't let anyone deceive you. Don't let the enemy try to give you his cheap imitations which we know as occult gifts. The gifts of the enemy will not bless you and they will certainly harm your spirit and your immortal soul. The real spiritual gifts all come in and through the Holy Spirit. They are given as God discerns their need in each of us. I encourage you to seek them now with all your heart. You can be certain that Father God is faithful to give you all you need to accomplish your purpose in the

Kingdom. Use your seer anointing to discover your Kingdom identity and always remember who the Lord says you are. Then pursue the path of love which will elevate you into His image. Trust the promise of Jesus in the passage below.

If you then, being evil, know how to give good gifts to your children, how much more will your heavenly Father give the Holy Spirit to those who ask Him! (Luke 11:13)

REMEMBER THIS
YOU ARE WHO GOD GIFTED YOU TO BE

PRAYER

For this reason we also, since the day we heard it, do not cease to pray for you, and to ask that you may be filled with the knowledge of His will in all wisdom and spiritual understanding; that you may walk worthy of the Lord, fully pleasing Him, being fruitful in every good work and increasing in the knowledge of God; strengthened with all might, according to His glorious power, for all patience and longsuffering with joy; (Colossians 1:9-11)

Chapter Eight

REVEALED IN YOUR
GIFTS OF POWER

This morning I spent time in the Word and then received a call from my wife Gloria who is celebrating New Year with her family in Korea. She was sharing testimonies of the amazing level of God's favor and blessings being manifested all around her. Believers are amazed and have started to testify, "That's God's favor!" Marginal believers are being strengthened in their faith and testifying to the favor of God. Unbelievers are being convinced by this mighty outpouring of favor. After this wonderful time of sharing testimonies of Jesus, I went upstairs to spend time with the Lord while I waited for my daughter, Michelle, to call and make sure I am okay. To tell the truth, I had sort of forgotten about what the Lord had promised for today.

As I went face down in the worship room, I was suddenly lifted up into His presence. I didn't see many things today, but what I saw was awesome. I was standing in front of the Lord and He had extended His right hand which was doubled up into a fist. This was something of a surprise. I didn't hear any words. So, I just focused my eyes on the right hand of the Lord. I was comforted to see that it was not a fist of anger, judgment, or punishment. It was closed gently and not tightly as from anger.

His thumb was prominently on top of His hand and I understood by the Spirit that His authority was over what was in His hand. Slowly, He opened His hand with palm up and displayed several items. I saw gold coins, a gold chain necklace with a small medallion, and a signet ring.

Suddenly, I remembered what the Lord had promised about releasing something awesome today, and there it was in His open right hand. For a short while, I just stood there staring at what He was holding. I didn't know if He was displaying something about Himself or releasing these things to us. So, I waited! Then the Lord extended His hand a little further indicating that He was releasing these things to those who had received the promise. I started to reach for them, but suddenly felt a twinge in my spirit not to just take them out of His hand. So, I extended my two hands with palms up and waited for the Lord to decide which part I might receive. He slowly and gently turned His hand over to release all of these into my hands (this is for you also).

I immediately understood from the Spirit that the gold coins represent a promise of increased and anointed provision in our lives and our ministries. The chain with a medallion is a symbol of the authority of the Lord being released to each one receiving it. It is to be worn on the outside of our garments so that others will see the authority and be more open to receive the ministry of the gospel accompanied by healings, miracles, signs and wonders. The signet ring is a symbol of standing in the office of the Lord and representing Him and the Kingdom of God in our ministry. I remembered the importance of the signet ring from the Biblical accounts of Joseph, Esther, Daniel, and Haggai. I meditated especially on the passage from Haggai 2:23, *"In that day,' says the Lord of hosts, 'I will take you, Zerubbabel My servant, the son of Shealtiel,' says the Lord, 'and will make you like a signet ring; for I have chosen you,' says the Lord of hosts."* You have been chosen to be like a signet ring of the Lord. You are the symbol of His authority and presence! Awesome! Amen?

I was in awe of what the Lord released today and I honestly thought it was more than enough for one visit. I mistakenly believed that the time of this visit was over. As we prepared to leave, I was surprised when the Lord released even more. As we stood up to leave His presence, the Lord came to each one and placed something like a cloak over the backs of each person. The cloaks were awesome and looked like the radiant glory of God. Then the Lord gave revelation knowledge about His plan to let His glory reside on you and to be visible to those who are being led by the Spirit. This too will be a sign which the Lord will place on you. It will also point to His coming again in great power and glory very soon!

I pray that you will be able to receive all these amazing gifts from the Lord! I pray that you will be able to carry the anointing, authority, provision, and glory He is releasing for you and your ministry! I pray that the Lord will reveal all of these things to you and that they will begin to manifest immediately in your life, work, and ministry! Amen and Amen! Praise the Lord! He is so good! Remember, "The Lord is good, and His mercy endures forever!" Hallelujah! Amen!!!!

THREE POWER GIFTS

> *...to another faith by the same Spirit, to another gifts of healings by the same Spirit, to another the working of miracles...*, (1 Corinthians 12:9-10)

If you agree with me that you are who you are gifted to be, then you should earnestly seek the gifts you need to accomplish God's plan for your life. Note that the Word of God directs you to desire spiritual gifts. Look again at what Paul wrote in 1 Corinthians 14:1, "*Pursue love, and desire spiritual gifts...*" If you are going to be all He created you to be, you need all the gifts which empower you to do the work assigned to you. It is right and proper for you to go for as many spiritual gifts as the

Lord allows. Trust me, He will not give you more than you need or more than He wants you to have.

At this point in your spiritual journey, you need to get free from all false humility. Real humility is being all that the Lord created you to be. It means that you have embraced who you are in Christ without being caught up in pride. After all, every gift and ability is from Him. It is completely un-natural for a believer to have no desire for spiritual gifts. It is God's will for you to first pursue love so that He can trust you to correctly use the additional gifts you are requesting. As your love grows, continue to press in to receive more spiritual gifts.

In this chapter, we will look closely at three spiritual gifts which are known as Gifts of Power. Notice that it is not about your power, but about the power of God working through you under the leadership and guidance of the Holy Spirit. All of these gifts are released to provide the power you need to work out your mission for the Kingdom. As your ministry expands, you will need more gifting to accomplish your mission. It is right and good for you to constantly seek more. I remind you of the promise in Psalm 115:14-15, *"May the Lord give you increase more and more, you and your children. May you be blessed by the Lord, Who made heaven and earth."* This is my prayer for you as you go through this study and as your gifts are activated and strengthened for His purpose in your life and for the fulfillment of your destiny in the Kingdom of God.

Think about this. It is completely appropriate for you to seek and expect to receive spiritual power. Remember what Jesus told the disciples in Luke 24:49, *"Behold, I send the Promise of My Father upon you; but tarry in the city of Jerusalem until you are endued with power from on high."* What is the primary purpose for this power? It is to enable you to be an effective witness. You can validate this in Acts 1:8, *"But you shall receive power when the Holy Spirit has come upon you; and you shall be witnesses to Me in Jerusalem, and in all Judea and Samaria, and to the end of the earth."* The Lord releases His power to you so that your witness will be effective as it is confirmed with miracles, signs and wonders. Now is a good time to seek and to wait for power from on high.

POWER GIFT ONE THE GIFT OF FAITH

...to another faith by the same Spirit...
1 Corinthians 12:9)

The spiritual gift of faith is much more than simple belief. Remember what was written in James 2:19, *"You believe that there is one God. You do well. Even the demons believe—and tremble!"* The faith given as a spiritual gift is filled with power and authority. This faith is the supernatural ability to believe without doubt. In the natural: people doubt first and later believe after they see the proof. The spiritual gift of faith does not originate in the natural nor does it emerge from within us. It is a definite supernatural gift of the Holy Spirit and is endued with the power released on the Day of Pentecost.

This faith is a gift which comes as a fulfillment of the promise in Joel 2:28-32. It is the next step beyond saving faith. Saving faith is given as a gift which gets you into the Kingdom of God. Look again at the description in Ephesians 2:8-9, *"For by grace you have been saved through faith, and that not of yourselves; it is the gift of God, not of works, lest anyone should boast."* The spiritual gift of faith gets the Kingdom of God into you. The gift of faith goes one step further than your original saving faith. It empowers you to believe without doubting so that you receive whatever you ask in Jesus' name.

> *But let him ask in faith, with no doubting, for he who doubts is like a wave of the sea driven and tossed by the wind. For let not that man suppose that he will receive anything from the Lord; he is*

a double-minded man, unstable in all his ways.
(James 1:6-8)

The gift of faith believes and receives the answer to your prayers even before they manifest in the natural. Supernatural faith is to believe you have the answer as soon as you pray. It is not dependent on seeing the outcome. Remember that spirit filled disciples do not go by what they see. They walk by faith and in the power gift of faith. Amen? Disciples with this kind of faith know that when Jesus cursed the fig tree, the roots were already dead before the tree showed its true condition. As soon as something manifests in the natural, it ceases to be based on faith. We believe it and receive it because we trust the Lord without reservation. This is the working of the gift of faith.

So Jesus answered and said to them, "Have faith in God. For assuredly, I say to you, whoever says to this mountain, 'Be removed and be cast into the sea,' and does not doubt in his heart, but believes that those things he says will be done, he will have whatever he says. Therefore I say to you, whatever things you ask when you pray, believe that you receive them, and you will have them."
Mark 11:22-24

The Bible is filled with examples of the gift of faith. By the gift of faith Jesus rested on a pillow during the storm. He already had the assurance they were going to safely arrive over on the other shore (Mark.4:35). Think about how the Lord can release powerful messages of assurance to you through the power gift of faith. When you know the outcome for you is going to be good, you don't need to fear the process of getting there. Ananias had the assurance that Saul (Paul) would receive the baptism of the Holy Spirit before he went to see him, (Acts 9). Faith involves action. Remember that faith without works is dead. Real faith is trust. When you have hope it is based on knowing that Jesus can do something. When you have the gift of faith, you know that He will do it. Notice this in action in the passage below.

> *So He asked his father, "How long has this been happening to him?" And he said, "From childhood. And often he has thrown him both into the fire and into the water to destroy him. But if You can do anything, have compassion on us and help us." Jesus said to him, "If you can believe, all things are possible to him who believes."* (Mark 9:21-23)

The child's father wondered if Jesus could heal his son. That wasn't the real issue in this situation. Jesus pointed to the real issue. Did the father believe that he would receive what he was asking? Then Jesus stated a very powerful truth. All things are possible to a person who has the gift of faith. How is your faith working in your life? Is it solid enough to release the power of God into your circumstances? Does your faith reach deeply into the truth that all things are possible with God? Challenge your gift with these questions. If you need more faith ask the Lord. He is always faithful to give you all the spiritual gifts you need to accomplish His purposes in your life. Trust Him implicitly. He keeps all His promises.

I heard someone say: Don't tell others what you believe you are going to receive until it manifests, because they will try to talk you out of it. At first glance, this may sound like good advice, but I think this is focused on your doubts rather than your faith. If you are truly operating in the power gift of faith, you will claim the results without any fear that someone else can take them away. Your faith is not dependent on what other people think or say. Your faith is based on your absolute trust that the Lord will give you whatever you need. He will give you whatever you ask in accordance with the name and mission of Jesus Christ. You can always count on Him. He will not let you down. Amen?

Consider this: you are known by how the power gift of faith is manifesting in your life and ministry. If you are faithless, others will see it. If you always hedge your prayers to avoid disappointment, people will take note of it. This gift is given so that your witness for the Lord will be strengthened. Even if others doubt the outcome, they will be transformed when they see the results. This is how you use your faith as a witness. As people see it at work in you, they will believe it is possible for them.

When we were moving from Texas to South Carolina, several real estate workers told us not to list our house for sale when the housing market was down. During worship, the Lord spoke to me. He asked: "Are you going to trust me or the market?" I made a firm decision to trust the Lord, and we listed our house for sale. The second family who looked at the house bought it. Shortly after this, the real estate agency asked us to speak at a prayer breakfast for their agency on living by faith. We were also given an opportunity to witness about living by faith to the agents who helped us purchase our new home. Your spiritual gift of faith is truly a powerful witness for the Lord. Use it well, and you will become known for who you are in Christ.

POWER GIFT TWO

When I shared a recent spiritual experience with others, I felt a need to begin by saying, "WOW!" The presence of the Lord has grown so much stronger since this past celebration of Rosh Chodesh! This morning, the power moving in the worship room was almost beyond my ability to handle. It is awesome and I just want to thank and praise the Lord because He has made it available to you and me. I pray that you will experience this awesome increase! The Lord began to show me people and ministries where His power is breaking out right now. I was carried in the Spirit to a church in South Korea and witnessed a mighty breakthrough of His Glory (Remember that this is available to you and your ministry as well). In the vision, I witnessed several extremely powerful releases of His Glory. They seemed to burst into the worship center and explode with power like a sun burst. The glory spread to everyone present in worship and each time it increased in intensity in their spirits. It was awesome and so powerful. There is a great elevation in their ability to host the Glory and the Lord is releasing more and more. Just when they think that this is all they can handle, He gives more. Hallelujah! Thank you Lord!

I was carried in the Spirit back to a room in heaven, and watched as the Lord did surgery on several people. First, I saw Him press His hand into the left side of a woman and remove something like a cancerous growth. If you or someone you know needs this today. Receive it by faith. Then I watched as He pressed into the left side of a man's chest and removed something from the lung which I understood to be a tumor. There is an anointing for tumors to be removed today. Reach out by faith and receive it in Jesus' Name. The Great Physician is in and He is doing some mighty works of healing today. As I watched, none of those receiving the surgery seemed to be in pain. They were wide awake and the Lord was doing it without anesthesia.

Then I saw a man kneeling before the Lord, and the Lord was reaching into the left side of the man's head. The Lord pulled something out of his head which was orange in color and about the size of a cherry tomato and it had many very long and thin roots that came out with it. At first, I was convinced that it was a brain tumor. There is an anointing today for brain tumors to disappear and healing to occur. Then the Lord revealed something to me in the Spirit. This was also called a root of bitterness. All these long roots had been spread through his mind and blocked what the Lord wanted to do for him. The Lord is standing ready today to remove every root of bitterness you are willing to let go. Don't miss this opportunity! Then the

Spirit told me that roots of bitterness are like cancer and they weaken the mind so that actual cancers can grow. These two things are all a part of the same spiritual problem. For our own sake we need to let the Lord remove it all. Amen?

All of these surgeries were happening on the left side of the people. I asked for revelation to understand this. It didn't come for a long time, but finally I got it. The right side is the side of authority. We can deal with the things in our area of authority. The Lord is dealing with things outside our area of authority today. I know that we should have this authority, but some of our spiritual challenges have left us a little short on faith in these areas which seem beyond us. Trust the Lord! You believe and He will do the work! Amen?

Then I saw several men moving so fast it was difficult to focus on them. I believe some of them were people and some were angels. They moved into a position surrounding the man still kneeling on the floor after his surgery. The Lord said, "I am sending people to be around you and help you to keep your healing! You will feel so much blessing that you will not be tempted to get back into bitterness! The hurt has been removed today so that you can open up to receive them and let yourself trust again!" Wow! Are you ready for this? My thoughts went to 1 Corinthians 13:1-3, *"Though I speak with the tongues of men and of angels, but have not love, I have become sounding brass or a clanging cymbal. And though I have the gift of prophecy, and understand all mysteries and all knowledge, and though I have all faith, so that I could remove mountains, but have not love, I am nothing. And though I bestow all my goods to feed the poor, and though I give my body to be burned, but have not love, it profits me nothing."*

Today is a good day to fall on your knees and pray in the Spirit to open the door to your heart and soul so the Lord can do this mighty work in you. Today is a good day to receive the healing anointing in these areas and minister it to others. I believe this is one of those days when we are not sure what to pray, but we know that the Holy Spirit will pray through us and make all things known to the Lord so that we can receive whatever healing we need. Amen!

GIFTS OF HEALINGS

...to another gifts of healings by the same Spirit...
(I Corinthians 12:9)

The spiritual "gifts of healings" are all pointing to supernatural healings. They are essentially done with no human assistance. At our best, we merely let these gifts flow through us by acknowledging that they are all works of the Lord. This passage speaks of "gifts of healings" because there are three unique categories of healings. There is a gift for physical healings for things like cancer, deafness, blindness, and etc. In addition there are gifts for emotional healings such as anxiety, stress, worry, fear and etc. In one of our meetings last year, someone was healed of claustrophobia. A third type of healing is spiritual healing for things like bitterness, un-forgiveness, jealousy, strife, and etc.

There are at least three unique ways the gifts are released. Sometimes a spoken word of knowledge will release the healing power. At other times it may be through touch such as laying on of hands or administering healing oil. Another way we often see these healings is as a direct manifestation of the glory of God. In the presence of His glory (*"kavod"* – weighty presence) people are healed by His spiritual touch without the assistance of any person. All we are asked to do in these cases is to set the environment and release our faith as we encourage those in need to trust Him for their healing.

These gifts of healings have important purposes in God's plan. In the Bible you can see these gifts bringing glory to God as in Mark 2:12, *"Immediately he arose, took up the bed, and went out in the presence of them all, so that all were amazed and glorified God...*" This should always be the outcome for those who witness the working of gifts of healings. If you are taking the glory, these gifts will not likely continue to manifest. As a spiritual leader operating in these gifts, it is your responsibility to always focus praise and glory to the Lord. There is always a danger that pride will manifest if you take credit for what the Lord is doing. Once this happens, you will likely be on a path toward a downfall.

You can also see the gifts of healings manifesting in order to confirm the Word of God as in Mark 16:20, *"And they went out and preached every-where, the Lord working with them and confirming the word through the accompanying signs. Amen."* We live in an age of doubt. As you go forth to minister in a culture of doubt, the Lord will release signs and wonders to confirm that your proclamation of the Gospel of the Kingdom is accurate and real. Expect the Lord to release spiritual gifts to accompany your ministry. He has always done this in the past. You can count on Him to do it in the present as well as in the future.

At other times these gifts provide the testimonies which build faith in others to accept your ministry and to make the choice to follow Jesus as in John 6:2, *"Then a great multitude followed Him, because they saw His signs which He performed on those who were diseased."* Jesus used a healing miracle to prove that he had the authority to forgive sins. Mark 2:10-12, *"But that you may know that the Son of Man has power on earth to forgive sins" He said to the paralytic "I say to you, arise, take up your bed, and go to your house." Immediately he arose, took up the bed, and went out in the presence of them all, so that all were amazed and glorified God, saying, "We never saw anything like this!"* Take a little time and note down some other ways these gifts have helped to confirm the work of Jesus and His disciples. Now, note how He has also done this in your ministry. It is always amazing to watch the Lord work this way. I love the way it manifested in the book of Acts.

And His name, through faith in His name, has made this man strong, whom you see and know. Yes, the faith which comes through Him has given him this perfect soundness in the presence of you all." (Acts 3:16)

The gifts of healings are for all of Jesus' disciples. They are as valid today as they were when Jesus was physically present on the earth. They are for all true believers and not just for some super apostles. Go back to the Gospel of John and study what Jesus said in chapters fourteen through seventeen. Focus particularly on what Jesus said in John 14:12, *"Most assuredly, I say to you, he who believes in Me, the works that I do he will do also; and greater works than these he will do, because I go to My Father."* Read this aloud over and over until it becomes a foundational principle in your faith. Do the same with John 17:20, *"I do not pray for these alone, but also for those who will believe in Me through their word;"* All these promises of Jesus are as much for you as for the original twelve. These promises are part of your mandate and gifting which Jesus released in the Great Commission.

And He said to them, "Go into all the world and preach the gospel to every creature. And these signs will follow those who believe: In My name they will cast out demons; they will speak with new tongues; they will take up serpents; and if they drink anything deadly, it will by no means hurt them; they will lay hands on the sick, and they will recover." (Mark 16:15, 17 and 18)

The bible is filled with examples of the gifts of healings at work in the ministry of Jesus and His disciples. The Four Gospels provide a long list of all the healings worked by Jesus. They also record the work of the disciples who were sent forth with the commission to preach and to heal. Luke chapter ten records the time when Jesus sent seventy disciples in addition to the original twelve. He told them to go out two by two. One of his instructions to them is recorded in Luke 10:9, *"And heal the sick there, and say to them, 'The kingdom of God has come near to you.'"* When they returned they gave praise to God and expressed their amazement at how these gifts had manifested in their ministry. This will happen for you as well. Believe it. Receive it and begin to minister it in the mighty name of Yeshua ha Messiach.

Philip was a deacon in the early church. He was not an apostle or prophet, he was a deacon, a servant of God. He was selected to give out supplies to the widows of Greek descent. That sounds like a very mundane task for a disciple, but this didn't hold Philip back or limit the flow of spiritual gifts in his ministry. You may see your commission in the kingdom as mundane at this time. Learn from Philip. Don't let that hold you back from ministering in the power gifts of healings. Your ministry will be confirmed in power just as his was. Notice how it is described in the passage below and then claim it for yourself.

> *And the multitudes with one accord heeded the things spoken by Philip, hearing and seeing the miracles which he did. For unclean spirits, crying with a loud voice, came out of many who were possessed; and many who were paralyzed and lame were healed.* (Acts 8:6-7)

POWER GIFT THREE THE WORKING OF MIRACLES

...to another the working of miracles... (1 Corinthians 12:10)

The word *miracle* comes from the Greek word *"dunamis."* Many English words are derived from this root word for power:

words like dynamo, dynamic, dynamite are based on that root word. *"Dunamis"* describes a very distinct and special kind of power. It is power and might that multiplies itself. This is the kind of working of miracles we are commissioned to do. When you let this spiritual gift flow through you it will provide a definite revelation of who you are in Christ. This kind of gift never comes from human ability. It is supernatural. It is a power gift of the Holy Spirit.

When Jesus told the disciples they would be endued with power, I don't believe they had any idea how powerful that gifting would be. The working of miracles is certainly supernatural. When these works manifest, people know that it is God who is at work because no human being could do these things. None of the other spiritual gifts are like miracles. A miracle happens when a missing eye is restored where none existed before. A miracle happens when fused vertebrae are suddenly replaced by brand new ones. When a missing limb or other body part grows back, that is a miracle. When people see real miracles of God, it opens their spirit to hear the Gospel of the Kingdom. You have been called to be there and speak it when they are ready to listen. Every time miracles occur, immediately proclaim the gospel again.

Miracles are always supernatural and therefore contrary to nature and natural law. They sometimes manifest in order to deliver people from danger whether it is from manmade problems or natural disasters. At times this power gift manifests in order to deliver people from demons or to release them from unholy captivity. People may even be delivered from their own rebellious actions. As you can see, miracles often manifest in order to lead people to accept the gospel and to be saved.

Miracles always have an important purpose in God's plan. At times they come to confirm the preaching of the Word of God as we see in John 5:36, *"But I have a greater witness than John's; for the works which the Father has given Me to finish—the very works that I do—bear witness of Me, that the Father has sent Me.*" At other times miracles manifest in order to build faith in the Word of God. They help people to see and believe that the Bible must be true. We see this happening in John 10:25, "*Jesus answered...The works that I do in My Father's name, they bear witness of Me.*" These accounts are much more than a list of old stories about things which happened in the past. They are testimonies to us of what the Lord can and will do now. It is important for you to understand that Jesus expects you to carry on His work. Like Him, you are to be carrying on the work of the Father. Read John 14:12-14. Read aloud the powerful passage below. Read it over and over until the promises become yours.

> *Most assuredly, I say to you, he who believes in Me, the works that I do he will do also; and greater works than these he will do, because I go to My Father. And whatever you ask in My name, that I will do, that the Father may be glorified in the Son. If you ask anything in My name, I will do it.*

The bible is filled with examples of the gift of miracles. In the Old Testament we see Elijah and Elisha raising the dead as a miraculous work of faith. In the New Testament we see Jesus doing the same things. In addition, you can see that through this same spiritual gift both Peter and Paul raised people from the dead. Think about it. Peter prayed and Dorcas (Tabitha) was raised from the dead. (Acts 9:39-43.) Paul raised a young man who died after a fall from a window (Acts 20:6-10). With this same gift Paul struck a false prophet blind.

> *And now, indeed, the hand of the Lord is upon you, and you shall be blind, not seeing the sun for a time. And immediately a dark mist fell on him,*

and he went around seeking someone to lead him by the hand. (Acts 13:11)

Jesus constantly healed the sick and did miracles. In fact He is the greatest miracle worker in human history. I say it in the present tense because this work has not ended. Remember what the writer said in Hebrews 13:8, *"Jesus Christ is the same yesterday, today, and forever."* He hasn't changed. His power has not diminished. His original commissioning for His disciples to do the same things and even greater things has not been rescinded or diminished over time. Now it is your turn to carry on His miraculous work. Are you ready for it? Use your gift of supernatural faith to fully believe and receive this commissioning.

I have often wondered why His church would assume that He has changed. Do we think he stopped caring for us after the ascension? I want to assure you that He has not lost His love for us nor has He stopped interceding for us. His desire is for you to move in the gifts of the Spirit and in power. He loved people so much that he healed them, set them free from demonic oppression, and raised them from the dead. He still loves people the same way today. If that changed, it would mean that the scriptures must be wrong. But, they are not wrong and He has not changed. Amen?

He commanded us to teach all His commands. Perhaps we should start by releasing the command He gave in Matthew 10:7-8, *"And as you go, preach, saying, 'The kingdom of heaven is at hand.' Heal the sick, cleanse the lepers, raise the dead, cast out demons. Freely you have received, freely give."* This is one of the commands He told us to both follow and teach. Do you believe this? Some people believe He said it, but they don't believe it is for them. This is tragic. If it is not possible to obey this command, why would Jesus ask us to teach it? It is true and we are given the gifts of the Spirit to confirm it for others.

Why was the Son of God manifested? The Word of God says that Jesus' purpose was to destroy the work of the Devil. Think about that as you read aloud over and over 1 John 3:8, *"For this purpose the Son of God was manifested, that He might destroy the work of the devil."* You are commissioned to do the same work. What is the work of the devil that we are to destroy? Jesus described it in John 10:10, *"The thief does not come except to steal, and to kill, and to destroy. I have come that they may have life, and that they may have it more abundantly."* In this verse, you can clearly see the difference between the work of Jesus and the work of the devil. Now consider this: Jesus told us to carry on His work. He said to do the same things he was doing and even greater works! Are you ready to carry this anointing?

Most people understand that Jesus has anointed us to proclaim the gospel of the Kingdom. The challenge often comes in believing the rest of that commissioning. He told us to heal the sick, raise the dead, cleanse lepers and cast out demons. That seems very clear in the Bible, but is it clear in your thinking? Is it empowering your ministry? Jesus expects us to be kingdom builders. Faithful disciples try to make earth like heaven. Why? That's what Jesus taught us to do. In Heaven, there is no sickness. No one is infirm. No one is oppressed by the devil in Heaven. We are to pray that it will be the same on earth. When we pray, we must believe that we will receive whatever we ask for. Jesus gave us a very definite prayer in Luke 11:2, *"So He said to them, "When you pray, say: Our Father in heaven, Hallowed be Your name. Your kingdom come. Your will be done on earth as it is in heaven."* Now He has commission you and me to make it happen.

I will say it again to make the point stronger. There are no sick people in heaven, therefore we can know with certainty that sickness is not God's will for us. There are no demon possessed people in heaven. There are no deformed bodies in heaven. These things are not a part of His will and have no place in His presence. Remember: It is all about the Kingdom of God, and it is all based on prayer! You should seek gifts and pray continuously to do His will. Remember, you are who you are gifted to be. Amen? Let the working of your gifts reveal it more clearly to you and expect them to be made manifest to others as a confirmation of the Gospel you proclaim.

Once again, I challenge you to take control of your own spirit and command your spiritual eyes and ears to be opened wider so that you can see who you are and what is happening in the spiritual realm now. To build your faith so that you can do this, read aloud again what Paul said in 1 Corinthians 14:32, *"And the spirits of the prophets are subject to the prophets."* You are not a helpless victim. You have spiritual authority (see Luke 10:19). You even have spiritual authority over you own spirit. Now is the time to take charge in order to activate and increase your seer anointing. Amen?

PRAYER

I pray for them. I do not pray for the world but for those whom You have given Me, for they are Yours. And all Mine are Yours, and Yours are Mine, and I am glorified in them. Now I am no longer in the world, but these are in the world, and I come to You. Holy Father, keep through Your name those whom You have given Me, that they may be one as We are. While I was with them in the world, I kept them in Your name. Those whom You gave Me I have kept; and none of them is lost except the son of perdition, that the Scripture might be fulfilled. But now I come to You, and these things I speak in the world, that they may have My joy fulfilled in themselves. I have given them Your word; and the world has hated them because they are not of the world, just as I am not of the world. I do not pray that You should take them out of the world, but that You should keep them from the evil one. They are not of the world, just as I am not of the world. Sanctify them by Your truth. Your word is truth. As You sent Me into the world, I also have sent them into the world. And for their sakes I sanctify Myself, that they also may be sanctified by the truth. "I do not pray for these alone, but also for those who will believe in Me through their word; that they all may be one, as You, Father, are in Me, and I in You; that they also may be one in Us, that the world may believe that You sent Me. And the glory which You gave Me I have given them, that they may be one just as We are one: I in them, and You in Me; that they may be made perfect in one, and that the world may know that You have sent Me, and have loved them as You have loved Me. (John 17:9-23)

Chapter Nine

REVEALED IN YOUR PROPHETIC GIFTS

As I entered the Lord's presence this morning, I went into an open vision. I was standing in front of a small round table covered with a simple white tablecloth. In the middle of the table was a gold chalice. Its design was very simple. There were no engravings or designs on the outside of the cup. Inside the cup I saw dark red wine which seemed to be moving by some unseen power. As it moved, the light reflected from it and drew my attention more and more. I thought about many of Jesus' "I AM" statements which seemed to be at the heart of this table, cup, wine, and bread as well as the light reflecting from the surface. "I AM the light of the world!" "I AM the bread of heaven!" "I AM the resurrection and the life!"

I reached out my hand to take the cup and suddenly everything in front of me seemed to disappear. I was suddenly being carried through the heavens at a great rate of speed. I was lifted up to an open meadow on the top of a low mountain. I have visited this place many times, however I learned something new about it this morning. The Lord called it, "The Mount of Revelation!" Then I remembered that every time I have been at this place the Lord has given me some new or a deeper understanding of His Word and His truth. As I thought about this, I heard the Lord say, "Many people don't think about My blood! There is still power in My blood!"

I began to hum the tune of the old hymn, "Nothing but the blood!" So many churches which are trying to be "seeker sensitive" have quit talking about the blood so they will not offend unbelievers. How will the seekers find what they are looking for if they miss the blood of Jesus? We can't compromise the message in an attempt to prevent people from being offended. People were offended when they heard the gospel directly from Jesus, and the same type of people will be offended today. But remember what Jesus said, "Jesus answered and said to them, *"Go and tell John the things you have seen and heard: that the blind see, the lame walk, the lepers are cleansed, the deaf hear, the dead are raised, the poor have the gospel preached to them. And blessed is he who is not offended because of Me."* (Luke 7:22-23) You have to get past the offense to get into the blessing.

This morning, as I reached for the blood in the chalice, heaven was opened and I was carried into His presence. This is how it has always been. It is through the blood of Jesus that we are redeemed. It is the covering of the blood which allows us into the secret place of the Most High God. "Nothing but the blood of Jesus" was able to do this in the past and "Nothing but the blood of Jesus" can do it today. We must all come to Him through the blood. Ephesians 2:13, *"But now in Christ Jesus you who once were far off have been brought near by the blood of Christ."* In the two passages below, consider the power, access and blessings given in the blood of Jesus.

> *"But if we walk in the light as He is in the light, we*
> *have fellowship with one another, and the blood*
> *of Jesus Christ His Son cleanses us from all sin."*
> (1 John 1:7)

"Therefore, brethren, having boldness to enter the Holiest by the blood of Jesus, by a new and living way which He consecrated for us, through the veil, that is, His flesh, and having a High Priest over the house of God, let us draw near with a true heart in full assurance of faith, having our hearts sprinkled from an evil conscience and our bodies washed with pure water." (Hebrews 10:19-22)

May we never be ashamed of or offended by the blood of Jesus! May we be sprinkled and covered in the only substance which can cover us for eternity! Covered with the blood, may we be allowed into His presence today and always! May we never neglect or undervalue the blood of Jesus! May we receive the spiritual gifts bought and paid for by the blood of Jesus! Amen!

THE PROPHETIC GIFTS

Having then gifts differing according to the grace that is given to us, let us use them: if prophecy, let us prophesy in proportion to our faith; or ministry, let us use it in our ministering; he who teaches, in teaching; he who exhorts, in exhortation; he who gives, with liberality; he who leads, with diligence; he who shows mercy, with cheerfulness. (Romans 12:6-8)

There are nine gifts of the spirit. For the purposes of this study, they are divided into three groups of three. In the previous two chapters, we have looked at the three "Gifts of Revelation" and the three "Gifts of Power." Now we will consider the three gifts of the spirit which can be called verbal gifts. All of these three spiritual gifts involve the use of speech as directed by the Holy Spirit. When they flow through your words, they are put into action by the Holy Spirit's power. This outcome does not occur when you are speaking casually or out of your own spirit.

The power of God is released when you are speaking the Word of God as directed by the Spirit. None of the Lord's words are ever wasted. None of His words ever fail to accomplish their purpose. There is great power released when you are speaking the Word of God. There are two very important cautions in this area. First, be certain that you are speaking the Lord's words and not your own. False prophets bring down fire upon themselves. Then, be careful what comes out of your mouth because of the spiritual power which will be released. Consider what the Lord said to the prophet Jeremiah,

> *They have lied about the Lord, and said, "It is not He. Neither will evil come upon us, nor shall we see sword or famine. And the prophets become wind, for the word is not in them. Thus shall it be done to them." Therefore thus says the Lord God of hosts: "Because you speak this word, behold, I will make My words in your mouth fire, and this people wood, and it shall devour them.*
> (Jeremiah 5:12-14)

In this age of grace the primary purposes of prophecy are to build up, strengthen and comfort the people of God. You may be directed by the Lord to release words of judgment, but never assume this on your own authority. You may wind up hurting rather than building up the body of Christ. You must always be aware of how powerful the Word of God is when you speak it. You must always handle your gift of prophesy as an awesome privilege to be used with wisdom. Remember Paul's instructions in 1 Corinthians 14:1. You must always pursue love first. It is the most powerful ingredient in your spiritual gifting and you must have it for the Lord to trust you with power gifts. Think about the Lord's declaration through the prophet Isaiah.

His word will never come back void. It will always accomplish what He speaks into being. Use the Word of God carefully and with deep awe and respect.

> *For as the rain comes down, and the snow from heaven, and do not return there, but water the earth, and make it bring forth and bud, that it may give seed to the sower and bread to the eater, so shall My word be that goes forth from My mouth; it shall not return to Me void, but it shall accomplish what I please, and it shall prosper in the thing for which I sent it.* (Isaiah 55:10-11)

VERBAL GIFT ONE THE GIFT OF PROPHECY

...to another prophecy... (1 Corinthians 12:10)

The word translated as "prophecy" in this passage is from the Greek word "*propheteuo*." This Greek word means to "speak for another." In a literal sense as it is used here, it means to be God's spokesperson or His ambassador in the world and to others. Paul made it clear that this spiritual gift is one of the most important ones (see 1 Corinthians 14:1, "*Pursue love, and desire spiritual gifts, but especially that you may prophesy.*") Prophecy as describe here means: speaking under the inspiration of God. It has a special place in the church which must not be denied.

Consider the emphasis Paul placed on prophecy in his letter to the church in Corinth as well as his message given in 1 Thessalonians 5:19-20, "*Do not quench the Spirit. Do not despise prophecies.*" Because of its importance as revealed in these passages, I am devoting one chapter specifically to this spiritual gift. The remaining two verbal gifts will be discussed in the next chapter. For now, let's take a closer look at this gift which we are directed to seek with the greatest zeal. You must not neglect or despise this gift if you want to fulfill your purpose in the Kingdom of God. This is one of the essential gifts which should be operating in every believer. Remember how Paul said, *"For you can all prophesy in turn so that everyone may be instructed and encouraged."* (1 Corinthians 14:31, NIV)

In these last days, it is critically important for the body of Christ to be operating in the gift of prophecy. We need to respond quickly and effectively in the rapidly changing situations which are occurring in the world today. This gift is made available by the Holy Spirit to all spirit filled believers. Some are more adept at it because they have developed it by use. Others have hesitated to use the gift and it has diminished. People often hesitate because of a spirit of fear. They fear they may be wrong about what they are saying or that people may not receive it well. You need to cast out every spirit of fear which would hinder your work for the Lord. Take Paul's advice in 2 Timothy 1:7, *"For God has not given us a spirit of fear, but of power and of love and of a sound mind."* If it doesn't come from the Lord, who do you think releases this spirit? It comes from the enemy with the purpose of hindering your work for the Lord. Ask the Lord to set you free from the fear of man today.

Prophecy can also mean: to foretell events or to speak under inspiration about the future. The Lord spoke of this in John 16:13, *"However, when He, the Spirit of truth, has come, He will guide you into all truth; for He will not speak on His own authority, but whatever He hears He will speak; and **He will tell you things to come**."* I often speak to the Spirit of truth and claim this promise for my ministry. I advise you to do the same. Ask the Holy Spirit to confirm the promises of Jesus in your life. Consider what Jesus said in John 16:14, *"He will glorify Me, for He will take of what is Mine and declare it to you."* These promises are for you right now. Claim them and activate and empower your prophetic gifting.

In the Hebrew language, the word translated as prophesy has a root meaning of: "to flow forth or to spring forth." This gift comes so that you can let the Word of God and the teachings of Jesus spring forth through you. Your mouth becomes like a spring of life giving water as His truth flows through your prophetic utterances. True prophesy always exalts Jesus as Savior and Lord! Revelation 19:10c, *"For the testimony of Jesus is the spirit of prophecy."* True prophesy is always in agreement with God's Word. Look at the passage below and understand the fullness of this word.

> *And so we have the prophetic word confirmed,*
> *which you do well to heed as a light that shines in*
> *a dark place, until the day dawns and the morning*
> *star rises in your hearts; knowing this first, that*
> *no prophecy of Scripture is of any private inter-*
> *pretation, for prophecy never came by the will*
> *of man, but holy men of God spoke as they were*
> *moved by the Holy Spirit.* (2 Peter1:19-21)

There are several reasons why prophecy is important in the church today. Most people can agree that it was a very significant part of the church in the New Testament, but many do not see the purpose for it in this generation. It is my firm belief that the gift of prophecy is as important for the body of Christ now as it was in New Testament times. In the paragraphs below, we will consider some of the important purposes of prophecy in the church today. First, consider what we have been looking at throughout this study. The Lord wants you to know who you are in Christ and to understand His plan for your service in the Kingdom of God. Prophecy is one of the primary ways the Lord reveals these things to you. This is another reason to be certain that you do not despise prophecy in the church.

One powerful use of prophecy was revealed in and through the life and work of the prophet Elisha. The Lord constantly warned him of the locations of enemy forces and their planned attacks and ambushes against Israel. The king of Aram was outraged when plan after plan was thwarted through Elisha's prophetic words. He was convinced the only way Israel could know his plans was by having a spy planted on his staff. As he vented his rage and spoke his threats, the members of his team were moved by fear. One staff officer saved the day by clarifying the situation. This is recorded in 2 Kings 6:12, *"And one of his servants said, 'None, my lord, O king; but Elisha, the prophet who is in Israel, tells the king of Israel the words that you speak in your bedroom.'"*

As in the days of Elisha, the Lord uses the gift of prophecy to warn and protect the church and individual believers of enemy plans. I have personally experienced this. When a rebellious spirit began to control the people in one church where I ministered some of the people began to gather in order to grumble and make threats. During this time the Lord gave me open visions in which I saw exactly who was doing this and where they were located when they were in rebellion. The visions were so clear that I saw details of people's homes which I had never visited. At that time, I described these homes to my wife, Gloria. Later when we were in their houses, we saw that they were exactly as I had seen them in the visions. The Lord does not approve of rebellion in the church and He uses the gift of prophecy to warn church leaders of the plans of the enemy being worked through vulnerable people.

Occasionally the gift of prophecy is used to speak new life into the church. When people have lost their zeal for the Lord, they may slowly slip into a kind of lethargy similar to spiritual death. Human reason is at times powerless to bring them back to vibrancy and usefulness. When your bones feel dry and useless, you need prophesy to awaken your spirit again. A word from the Lord can breathe life back into a hopeless person or group. The Lord releases exactly the words needed to produce a positive result. These prophetic words are not likely to make sense in the arena of worldly wisdom. They transcend worldly wisdom in order to release the power of God into a seemingly hopeless situation. This is shown very clearly in the ministry of the prophet Ezekiel.

> *The hand of the LORD came upon me and brought me out in the Spirit of the LORD, and set me down in the midst of the valley; and it was full of bones. Then He caused me to pass by them all around, and behold, there were very many in the open valley; and indeed they were very dry. And He said to me, "Son of man, can these bones live?" So I answered, "O Lord GOD, You know." Again He said to me, "Prophesy to these bones, and say to them, 'O dry bones, hear the word of the Lord!*
> (Ezekiel 37:1-4)

Prophesy is used by the Lord to build us up and strengthen our spirits. Paul spoke of this to the Corinthian church in 1 Corinthians 14:3, *"But he who prophesies speaks **edification** and **exhortation** and **comfort** to men."* Considering this message from Paul, I understand that one of the Lord's primary uses of prophecy in the church can be summed up as the release of a word to edify, exhort, and comfort. This type of prophetic word is given to inspire the body of Christ to be ready for a spiritual renewal. It can also challenge believers to be rededicated to the work of the Gospel. This kind of prophetic utterance can also give people comfort in knowing that they are still surrounded by God's love.

Prophecy is a gift of the Spirit to provide guidance and counsel. Spirit led people receive prophetic words to tell them where to go as well as when and how to make the journey. Along the way, words of prophecy come to keep you in the safe paths of the Lord and to warn you of hazards and dangers along the way. Prophecy of this nature may also let you know when you should not go in a particular direction or to a particular place. If you desire to be Spirit led, you need to earnestly seek this gift. By this gift you will be enabled to know when you are called and where you are being sent by the Lord.

> *Now in the church that was at Antioch there were certain prophets and teachers: Barnabas, Simeon who was called Niger, Lucius of Cyrene, Manaen who had been brought up with Herod the tetrarch, and Saul. As they ministered to the Lord and fasted, the Holy Spirit said, "Now separate to Me Barnabas and Saul for the work to which I have called them." Then, having fasted and prayed, and laid hands on them, they sent them away.* (Acts 13:1-3)

In both the Old Testament and the New Testament the Holy Spirit spoke through prophets. One problem in the church today is that most people in what we call the mainline churches will not accept this kind of guidance. When people make this choice, they lose one of the powerful ways available for the Holy Spirit to lead them. You must not make this mistake. Remember Paul's counsel to the church that it must not *despise prophecies*." Look again at the prophecy the Lord gave through Joel and consider how Peter interpreted what was happening in the church on the Day of Pentecost. We are living in these last days, and we need to take seriously what the Lord has spoken to us in both the Old and New Testaments. Amen?

> *But this is what was spoken by the prophet Joel: "And it shall come to pass in the last days, says God, that I will pour out of My Spirit on all flesh; your sons and your daughters shall prophesy, your young men shall see visions, your old men shall dream dreams. And on My menservants and on*

My maidservants I will pour out My Spirit in those days; and they shall prophesy." (Acts 2:16-18)

Look again at how Peter saw the events of the Day of Pentecost as a fulfillment of this well know Biblical prophecy. The word of the Lord given through Joel seemed to be a perfect description of what the Lord was doing for them. Think about it. Biblically, when are the last days? These are the last days and this prophecy is for you and me. We need to understand the times and know what the body of Christ should do. We should be like the sons of Issachar. Remember what was said of them in 1 Chronicles 12:32, "*...the sons of Issachar who had understanding of the times, to know what Israel ought to do,*" Do you understand the times? Has the Lord revealed to you what the body of Christ should be doing in these times? Earnestly desire the spiritual gift of prophecy so that you can be wise in the Spirit. Remember that worldly wisdom is coming to nothing in these days.

John felt the urgency of this time more than most. In 1 John 2:18, he wrote, "*Little children, it is the last hour; and as you have heard that the Antichrist is coming, even now many antichrists have come, by which we know that it is the last hour.*" One of the Lord's powerful promises for this time (the last days) is a great outpouring of the gift of prophesy. This gift is being poured out on all flesh. Prophesy should be a common gift in the church today. Some today contend that prophecy ended with John the Baptist and Jesus. This idea is contrary to the written Word of God in the New Testament. Twenty three prophets are mentioned by name and references are made to entire groups of prophets working in the New Testament Church.

And in these days prophets came from Jerusalem to Antioch. Then one of them, named Agabus, stood up and showed by the Spirit that there was going to be a great famine throughout all

*the world, which also happened in the days of
Claudius Caesar.* (Acts 11:27-28)

From this and other passages, it is clear that prophets were
common in the New Testament Church into the second and third
generations. For example, Paul found disciples in Ephesus who
had never heard of the Holy Spirit. He knew this because of the
absence of spiritual gifts in these men. This all changed when
they were baptized in the Holy Spirit. Paul described it this
way in Acts 19:5-7, *"When they heard this, they were baptized
in the name of the Lord Jesus. And when Paul had laid hands
on them, the Holy Spirit came upon them, and they spoke with
tongues and prophesied. Now the men were about twelve in all."*
Twelve ordinary believers received these two gifts of the Spirit;
tongues and prophesy. An absence of gifts points to the need
for Holy Spirit baptism.

Many people try to limit what the Lord plans to do in these
last days. It is difficult to imagine, but many churches still practice discrimination against women. They have a firm belief that
this gift is not for females. Speaking through the prophet Joel,
the Lord made it clear that daughters would also prophesy.
Study carefully what Paul is saying in Galatians 3:28, *"There
is neither Jew nor Greek, there is neither slave nor free, there
is neither male nor female; for you are all one in Christ Jesus."*
Notice the inclusiveness of the gift of prophecy in Acts 21:8-9,
*"On the next day we who were Paul's companions departed and
came to Caesarea, and entered the house of Philip the evangelist, who was one of the seven, and stayed with him. Now this
man had four virgin daughters who prophesied."*

Why aren't we seeing this more in the church today? Have
we made the mistake of despising this gift? As you open up to
being led by the Spirit, expect gifts of prophesy to be released
to you and your church. I believe that we should be praying
intently for this gift to be restored. According to Paul, who
should seek it? 1 Corinthians 14:1, *"Pursue love, and desire*

spiritual gifts, but especially that you may prophesy." In reality, prophesy is the gift we should seek with the most zeal. Are you pressing in to receive more of this gift? In some groups I wonder if they have ever prayed for this gift. We need to heed Paul's advice given again in 1 Corinthians 14:39a, *"Therefore, brethren, desire earnestly to prophesy,"*

CHRISTIAN DISCIPLES SHOULD EXPECT THESE GIFTS

But one and the same Spirit works all these things, distributing to each one individually as He wills. (1 Corinthians 12:11)

We know the source of the gift of prophecy. The Holy Spirit is the Father's designated source of the spiritual gift of prophesy. I believe that it is the will of the Lord for everyone in the body of Christ to receive this powerful gift through the work of the Holy Spirit in the church today. The Holy Spirit is the only legitimate source of true Biblical prophecy. Do not look to any other source.

As you know, the enemy tries to counterfeit everything coming from the Lord. His counterfeits are merely cheap copies of the real thing. Occult gifts coming through familiar spirits released by the enemy always produce the opposite of the promised fruit in the Word of God. If the gift of prophecy is to build up, the gift of the enemy is released to tear down. If the gift of the Spirit is to bring life, the enemy tries to release a spirit of death. If prophesy is meant to bring comfort, the gift of the enemy is judgment and condemnation. Never accept imitations of these spiritual gifts. The only source for the real thing is the Holy Spirit.

Spiritual gifts are released individually by the Holy Spirit. Consider this: God is not a stingy giver. He desires to equip each disciple with every gift needed for serving Him. That is

His plan and purpose for you. You have been instructed to desire and to seek spiritual gifts. If you have not been desiring gifts, you need to change. God gives to those who earnestly seek. In the body of the church, all the spiritual gifts should be present. In the passage below, notice that the writer is giving a word of exhortation for second generation believers.

> *Therefore we must give the more earnest heed to the things we have heard, lest we drift away. For if the word spoken through angels proved stead-fast, and every transgression and disobedience received a just reward, how shall we escape if we neglect so great a salvation, which at the first began to be spoken by the Lord, and was confirmed to us by those who heard Him, God also bearing witness both with signs and wonders, with various miracles, and gifts of the Holy Spirit, according to His own will?* (Hebrews 2:1-4)

The absence of gifts in the church should lead us to repentance. It should be a signal to us that we need to help the body of Christ return to its first love. Be an intercessor for the body of Christ. Earnestly desire spiritual gifts for others. Pray intentionally and persistently for spiritual gifts so that you can produce more fruit for the Kingdom of God. Paul gave very sound advice to His spiritual son, Timothy. I urge you to take this advice to heart in your own life and ministry. It was good advice then and it is still good for you and me.

> *For this reason I remind you to fan into flame the gift of God, which is in you through the laying on of my hands. For God did not give us a spirit of timidity, but a spirit of power, of love and of self-discipline.* (2 Timothy 1:6-7, NIV)

According to Paul, one of the ways gifts are imparted is through the laying on of hands. Certain conditions will limit the impartation of gifts. Unbelief will totally block the impartation. Un-forgiveness and strife will most certainly hinder the impartation of spiritual gifts. Fear produces an unreceptive heart. Right now decree that all these things which block or hinder the flow of spiritual gifts will be broken off from you and your church. Use the powerful words of scripture to empower your decrees. Remember that there is no fear in perfect love.

> *There is no fear in love; but perfect love casts out fear, because fear involves torment. But he who fears has not been made perfect in love.* (1 John 4:18)

I have been challenged by many people who do not believe that we can impart spiritual gifts. I remind them to check this out based on Paul's teaching in Romans 1:11-12, *"For I long to see you, that I may impart to you some spiritual gift, so that you may be established—that is, that I may be encouraged together with you by the mutual faith both of you and me."* The key thing to remember is that you are not the source of the gifts. The Holy Spirit is the only source of these gifts, however He has always used people's hands as a means of imparting them. Remember how Paul did this in the Church of Corinth.

Try not to get caught up in looking for all the reasons why things will not work. Focus on the possibilities inherent in the body of Christ. Nothing is impossible for God. On the other hand, all things are possible with Him. Seek out the possibilities. The Lord is always ready to break out of any box we place Him into. There is so much more creativity in the possibilities than in the limitations. God is creative by nature, and we were made in His image. Remember what He said about Himself in Revelation 21:5, *"Then He who sat on the throne said, 'Behold, I make all things new.' And He said to me, 'Write, for these words are true and faithful.'"* We too should be creative and expect new things to manifest constantly. After all, we are in the family business of making things new. Amen?

A sincere and receptive heart is the key to the effective impartation of spiritual gifts. If you desire the gift of prophecy, through the laying on of hands, I invite you to receive it today. You don't have to wait for a man or woman of God to release this to you. This is a gift of the Holy Spirit and He can impart it to you right now. Just ask the Lord. He is so good and so faithful to keep all His promises. These gifts of the Spirit are among those promises. Believe and receive them right now. Then give Him thanks and praise until they manifest.

PRAYER

Therefore I also, after I heard of your faith in the Lord Jesus and your love for all the saints, do not cease to give thanks for you, making mention of you in my prayers: that the God of our Lord Jesus Christ, the Father of glory, may give to you the spirit of wisdom and revelation in the knowledge of Him, the eyes of your understanding being enlightened; that you may know what is the hope of His calling, what are the riches of the glory of His inheritance in the saints, and what is the exceeding greatness of His power toward us who believe, according to the working of His mighty power which He worked in Christ when He raised Him from the dead and seated Him at His right hand in the heavenly places, far above all principality and power and might and dominion, and every name that is named, not only in this age but also in that which is to come. (Ephesians 1:15-21)

Chapter Ten

REVEALED IN YOUR VERBAL GIFTS

We are in a season of training and equipping, but this season is drawing to a close. The season of moving out into the harvest fields in a renewed and more powerful way has already opened. People have been holding back long enough, and for some too long. We are not called to find a cave in which to hide, but to boldly move forth to spread the Gospel of the Kingdom. This morning, I saw many people being urged to leave the safety and comfort of the classroom in Heaven and get back to the business of winning souls and preparing the bride of Christ. This morning, I asked the Lord to confirm His message by giving it to me a second time and this is what He did.

I went into an open vision for a second time and found myself standing at a bus stop on a busy street corner. A young black woman was standing between us and the bus which had stopped and opened the door. She was dressed in a bright purple sequined dress. The dress was long and the sleeves of the dress were long. It had an open collar but was only cut about an inch below her neck. She was wearing a gold scarf around her neck which was very long and wider than normal. It seemed too warm to wear a scarf on a day like today, but she was pulling it tightly around her neck. There was something special about this scarf. This is one of the reasons why I asked for a confirmation. I wanted to be certain that I had an understanding of the meaning of this article of clothing.

Then it came to me by revelation knowledge. This was a very special mantle of the Lord like the one we are told he will wear: *"Righteousness will be his belt and faithfulness the <u>sash</u> around his waist."* (Isaiah 11:5) The priestly garments include a linen sash, but it is of a different color. The one which is gold belongs to the Lord Himself as described in Revelation 1:12-13, *"I turned around to see the voice that was speaking to me. And when I turned I saw seven golden lampstands, and among the lampstands was someone "like a son of man," dressed in a robe reaching down to his feet and with a <u>golden sash</u> around his chest."* The sash worn by the woman in my vision was too big to be worn around her waist. So, she was wearing it like a scarf. She was being sent forth in royal colors and with this very special mantle from the Lord to be a Kingdom representative.

As we watched, she hesitated to get on the bus. She started back our way, but we all encouraged her to get on the bus. She continued to delay in spite of our words of encouragement. Many people are carrying powerful spiritual gifts, awesome mantles, and splendid signs of kingdom authority, but are hesitating in this hour to step out into their destiny. It is time to move. As we watched, the bus driver closed the door and started to drive away. We all called to the young woman and insisted that she get on the bus. She seemed so young and so vulnerable, and I wanted to go with her to support what the Lord planned for her to do, but the Lord would not allow it. He said, "It is time to let people move out of the safety and security of their places of training and fulfill their destiny! You must trust me and let them go! The time has come! You must not hesitate any longer!" The woman summoned her courage and started to run to catch up with the bus. She shouted to the driver and he finally stopped to let her in. Then the door closed and the bus drove out of sight.

After the Lord took us back to the classroom, many people were handed the things they needed for their assigned mission and then escorted to the door. They were given a gentle push and launched into their assigned mission field. I watched as men and women from many different nations, ethnic backgrounds, and age groups were launched from the classroom of Heaven. Are you feeling the gentle push of the Lord today? Is the Lord sending you forth to your mission field? The time to hesitate is over. It is time to leave the security of the nest and learn to fly under kingdom authority and power. This is your time! 10, 9, 8, 7, 6, 5, 4, 3, 2, 1, 0, Lift Off! Be launched now! I heard the Lord say, "*Go therefore and make disciples of all the nations, baptizing them in the name of the Father and of the Son and of the Holy Spirit, teaching them to observe all things that I have commanded you; and lo, I am with you always, even to the end of the age.*" (Matthew 28:19-20) Then I was launched. How about you! Ready, set, GO! Amen?

TWO ADDITIONAL VERBAL GIFTS

It is important for you to know who you are in Christ in order to be fully released in your anointing, authority and purpose for the Kingdom God. The Lord is very willing to reveal these truths to you. It is your responsibility to be willing to allow Him to do this for you. The main purpose for this book is to help you see and become who you truly are in Christ Jesus. The Lord wants you to see clearly how He sees you. He wants you to realize all the potential He created in you. His plans for you are actually better than your plans for yourself.

In the previous chapter, we explored the first verbal gift: prophesy. You saw how this gift can be used in a variety of ways in your service for the Lord. One of the uses of the gift is to help you clearly see your purpose and destiny in the Kingdom of God. This mystery can be revealed through the work of the Holy Spirit in and through you. Now is the time to fully realize the benefits of being Spirit-led. In the passage below, notice that spiritual gifts can be imparted through the laying on of hands.

> *And it happened, while Apollos was at Corinth, that Paul, having passed through the upper regions, came to Ephesus. And finding some disciples he said to them, "Did you receive the Holy Spirit when you believed?" So they said to him, "We have not so much as heard whether there is a Holy Spirit." And he said to them, "Into what then were you baptized?" So they said, "Into John's baptism." Then Paul said, "John indeed baptized with a baptism of repentance, saying to the people that they should believe on Him who would come after him, that is, on Christ Jesus." When they heard this, they were baptized in the name of the Lord Jesus. And when Paul had laid hands on them, the Holy Spirit came upon them, and they spoke with tongues and prophesied. Now the men were about twelve in all.* (Acts 19:1-7)

These twelve men in Ephesus had not yet come to an understanding of who they could be in Christ. A giant step was made in that direction when they received the Holy Spirit and began to operate in two of the powerful spiritual gifts. One of the first spiritual gifts they received was the vocal gift of prophesy which we discussed at length in the previous chapter. The second spiritual gift they received was also a verbal gift. It was the gift of speaking in tongues. This gift has often been misunderstood by the church. There are possibly more false teachings about this gift than any other. It is important to understand these gifts if you are going to operate in them and minister through them. Think about this and what the Lord wants for you as you study in more detail these next two spiritual gifts.

VOCAL GIFT TWO DIFFERENT KINDS OF TONGUES

...to another different kinds of tongues...
(1 Corinthians 12:10)

As I stated earlier, this is an often misunderstood gift. So, how should we begin to understand it? Think about this: everything broken in the fall of man in the Garden of Eden was corrected through Christ. In the Tower of Babel incident, the Lord sent a diversity of tongues in order to separate the people and frustrate their plans to usurp His authority. On the Day of Pentecost, the Lord used a diversity of tongues to bring people together. After receiving this gift, the disciples stood together in agreement for the first time. This resulted in them having favor with the people which brought a daily increase in their numbers.

So continuing daily with one accord in the temple, and breaking bread from house to house, they ate their food with gladness and simplicity of heart, praising God and having favor with all the people. And the Lord added to the church daily those who were being saved. (Acts 2:46-47)

This gift of the indwelling Holy Spirit is an important part of God's plan for your life and for the life of the church. When this gift is not present, people will see what Paul saw in Ephesus. The gifts of the Spirit were not manifesting because the baptism of the Holy Spirit had not come to these believers. As soon as they were baptized and Paul laid his hands on them the Holy Spirit came to them and released spiritual gifts through them. Forget about any false teachings which try to limit these gifts. Look at what Peter said on the Day of Pentecost and claim the promise for yourself. Think about it. This gift is to *you and to your children, and to all who are afar off, as many as the Lord our God will call.*" Study it for yourself in the passage below.

> *Then Peter said to them, "Repent, and let every*
> *one of you be baptized in the name of Jesus Christ*
> *for the remission of sins; and you shall receive*
> *the gift of the Holy Spirit. For the promise is*
> *to you and to your children, and to all who are*
> *afar off, as many as the Lord our God will call."*
> (Acts 2:38-39)

A few years ago during a conference, a woman came to us several times asking us to pray for her to be baptized in the Holy Spirit. She had one condition with her request. She insisted that we must not impart the spiritual gift of *"different kinds of tongues."* She was a very well educated person in worldly wisdom and possessed more than one professional degree. She had an established clinical practice and spent much of her time counseling others. She didn't want to be embarrassed in her professional setting because of speaking in tongues. She was a regular church goer, but understood clearly that she had never been baptized in the Holy Spirit. We explained to her that we don't make these decisions. Each of the spiritual gifts is given in accordance with the will of the Holy Spirit. Over and over, she made the decision not to receive Holy Spirit baptism because we could not assure her that she would not speak in tongues.

During one of the conference sessions, the man seated behind her stood up and began to roar (scream) at the top of his lungs. Each scream was long, piercing and extremely loud. Over and over, he screamed over her. We didn't understand this until she came to us after that session. A spiritual breakthrough came for her during those screams. She was now willing to trust the Holy Spirit to gift her any way He chose. My wife, Gloria, and I held her hands and prayed in the spirit. Suddenly something powerful hit her spirit. She began to exercise the gift of tongues. She prayed in the Spirit for a long time. Then she began to prophesy. After a short while, she began to see prophetic visions and released words of prophecy given to her by the Lord. We witnessed an amazing transition in this woman when she finally trusted the Holy Spirit to have His will in her life.

Have you let the Holy Spirit have His will over your life? Have you trusted Him to give you what He knows you need? Are you letting a tradition of man or a false teaching prevent you from experiencing the power of God in your life? If so, it is time to let go and let the Holy Spirit work through you. If you have been in a tradition which rejects the spiritual gift of tongues, it is time to let go of the traditions of man and be obedient to the commands of the Lord. If you have doubts about the gift of tongues, study the verse below and see what the Lord is saying to you in this passage. It is time to become the person you are in God's eyes.

> *Therefore, brethren, desire earnestly to prophesy, and do not forbid to speak with tongues.* (1 Corinthians 14:39)

THREE TYPES OF TONGUES

The Bible describes three (3) different types of tongues. To respond properly to the Holy Spirit, it is important for you to know and understand the use of all three. It is important for you to be open to any or all of these types of tongues. Power from on high brings these gifts to you and it is an insult to the Lord to refuse them. If you are going to become who God has called you to be, you must be obedient and let Him have His will in your life. If He wants you to have the spiritual gift of different tongues, be open to receive it. I believe that this gift is essential to your spiritual development.

1. A GIFT TO SPEAK TO GOD

The first type of tongues to consider is an unknown tongue unto God. In reality this is probably the most important type of tongues. Yet, it is probably the least well known of the three types. Paul describes it in the passage below. Study this passage and ask the Spirit of truth to guide you in more fully understanding the message for you. Then ask Him to impart this gift to you so that you can more fully live up to your potential in the Kingdom. If you are already flowing in this gift, ask for more.

> *For he who speaks in a tongue does not speak to men but to God, for no one understands him; however, in the spirit he speaks mysteries.* (1 Corinthians 14:2)

This type of tongue is given to edify the believer who possesses the gift. Paul teaches this in 1 Corinthians 14:4, *"He who speaks in a tongue edifies himself."* This type of tongue is given to assist you in prayer. Have you ever gone through a time so laden with emotion that you find it difficult to pray? Have you been caught up in a situation with so many possibilities that you don't know which one to choose? Have you ever felt that the enemy is oppressing you and seems to know in advance what you plan? Does it seem like Satan is getting the jump on your spiritual progress? If you answered yes to any of these questions, this type of tongues is for you.

> *Likewise the Spirit also helps in our weaknesses. For we do not know what we should pray for as we ought, but the Spirit Himself makes intercession for us with groanings which cannot be uttered. Now He who searches the hearts knows what the mind of the Spirit is, because He makes intercession for the saints according to the will of God.* (Romans 8:26-27)

This type of spiritual gift of tongues is used by the Lord to stir up the prophetic ministry. The Lord allows the Spirit to speak God's Word as a prophetic utterance in you as well as through you to others. This gift often comes in order to give you a confirmation of the Word you have already spoken. This particular type of the gift of tongues is often used by the Lord to refreshes your soul. It may also be released through you to bring refreshing to another individual or to the church.

> *For with stammering lips and another tongue He will speak to this people, to whom He said, "This is the rest with which You may cause the weary to rest," and, "This is the refreshing"; yet they would not hear.* (Isaiah 28:11-12)

This type of tongue gives you a victory over the devil. The enemy has no idea what you are saying when you use this gift of tongues. He has no idea what the Spirit is releasing for others through you. Paul encourages all believers to use this gift regularly. See Ephesians 6:18, *"praying always with all prayer and supplication in the Spirit,"* The various gifts of tongues are given to help you worship more effectively. When this gift comes you are literally worshipping in Spirit and truth.

> *For if I pray in a tongue, my spirit prays, but my understanding is unfruitful. What is the conclusion then? I will pray with the spirit, and I will also pray with the understanding. I will sing with the spirit, and I will also sing with the understanding.* (1 Corinthians 14:14-15)

2. A KNOWN TONGUE AS A SIGN TO UNBELIEVERS

> *And when this sound occurred, the multitude came together, and were confused, because everyone heard them speak in his own language.* (Acts 2:6)

On the Day of Pentecost the gift of tongues given to the disciples opened the way for over three thousand people to come to a saving knowledge of the gospel and to accept Yeshua as their Lord. Paul speaks to this type of tongues in 1 Corinthians 14:22, *"Therefore tongues are for a sign, not to those who believe but to unbelievers; but prophesying is not for unbelievers but for those who believe."* You see clearly in this teaching that you need both the gift of prophesy and the gift of tongues in order to fulfill your God given purpose. Each of these gifts has its place. Both are necessary for you to be complete in your gifting for the Lord's work. Embrace both gifts and pray that the Holy Spirit will always give you the wisdom to know which one to use in any particular circumstance.

On a visit to Israel, I was praying with my head touching the Western Wall. I was inside the area where many Orthodox Jewish men gather. I was praying aloud in the Spirit for a long time. I didn't know if what I was doing would be accepted in this area. To my surprise, one of the men in a black suit wearing a black hat (obviously an Orthodox Jewish man) approached me and wanted to talk. Fortunately he spoke English. After finishing this conversation, I walked away marveling at the outcome the Lord had worked through the gift of praying in the Spirit. Suddenly, I heard the Spirit telling me that He had been praying through me in Hebrew. In so doing, He opened a way for me to share with the Jewish man.

I often wonder how many opportunities for witnessing people have missed because they have not been open to receiving this type of gift from the Holy Spirit. If you want to be who you were create and destined to be, you need to allow the Holy Spirit to gift you in accordance with His will. Become the person He can use to witness to others. Become the person He chooses to speak through in order to release a powerful word in season as He reveals it to you. Become more like the Apostle Paul who could truthfully say, *"I thank my God I speak with tongues more than you all;"*

3. A TONGUE TO EDIFY THE CHURCH

The third unique type of tongue is one which is only understood through the assistance of an interpreter. This type of tongue is given in order to edify the church and must be accompanied by interpretation. When the interpretation is released, it may come through the original speaker or through another person with this spiritual gift. In the passage below avoid getting caught up in the argument concerning which gift is better. Focus on the main point. This gift is for the edification of the church.

> *I wish you all spoke with tongues, but even more that you prophesied; for he who prophesies is greater than he who speaks with tongues, unless indeed he interprets, that the church may receive edification.* (I Corinthians 14:5)

The gift of tongues is a "free will" gift. The Holy Spirit doesn't force anyone to speak in tongues. This spiritual gift is received by faith. Remember that faith is also a gift from the Holy Spirit. It is important to note that this is primarily a gift for ministry. Because it is a "free will gift," a person may neglect it as with any other spiritual gift. Paul cautions us not to do this in 1 Timothy 4:14, "*Do not neglect the gift that is in you, which was given to you by prophecy with the laying on of the hands of the eldership.*"

The Bible makes it clear that you may also stir up a spiritual gift as an act of your own will. Study carefully Paul's instructions to his spiritual son in 2 Timothy 1:6, "*Therefore I remind you to stir up the gift of God which is in you through the laying on of my hands.*" Remember that you are first told to desire gifts and to seek them. Look again at this teaching in 1 Corinthians 14:1, "*Pursue love, and desire spiritual gifts,*" I will let Paul give you the conclusion for his teachings about the spiritual gift of tongues in the passage below.

*What is the conclusion then? I will pray with the
spirit, and I will also pray with the understanding.
I will sing with the spirit, and I will also sing with
the understanding.* (I Corinthians 14:15)

Before completing this part of the teaching, I want to mention one other type of tongue. I did not go into detail about it because there is only one reference to it in scripture. I want you to be fully informed about tongues in this teaching, therefore I mention this one additional passage. The passage is very familiar to most believers, but I have never heard anyone discus this element of the passage. Consider what Paul wrote in 1 Corinthians 13:1, *"Though I speak with the tongues of men and of angels, but have not love, I have become sounding brass or a clanging cymbal."* Angels have their own unique language, and Paul indicates that some people may be gifted to understand what they are saying.

On one occasion, we heard angels talking when a group of people were in our home worship room. We had often heard them singing, but this was the first time we heard them speaking. When I heard it, I asked the other people present if they were hearing the angels. Everyone affirmed that they were hearing the angels talking to one another. I asked the Lord for the gift to interpret what they were saying, and the Lord gave it to me at that time. I understood clearly the last few sentences in their conversation. I have not heard anyone else speak of hearing this, but I felt it would be negligent to fail to mention it in this teaching. You can also ask the Lord for this spiritual gift.

EXAMPLES FROM SCRIPTURE

1. THE INTIAL OUTPOURING OF GIFTS

*When the Day of Pentecost had fully come, they
were all with one accord in one place. And*

suddenly there came a sound from heaven, as of a rushing mighty wind, and it filled the whole house where they were sitting. Then there appeared to them divided tongues, as of fire, and one sat upon each of them. And they were all filled with the Holy Spirit and began to speak with other tongues, as the Spirit gave them utterance. (Acts 2:1-4)

2. IN THE HOUSE OF A GENTILE BELIEVER

While Peter was still speaking these words, the Holy Spirit fell upon all those who heard the word. And those of the circumcision who believed were astonished, as many as came with Peter, because the gift of the Holy Spirit had been poured out on the Gentiles also. For they heard them speak with tongues and magnify God. (Acts 10:44-46)

3. BELIEVERS FROM APOLLOS' MINISTRY

And it happened, while Apollos was at Corinth, that Paul, having passed through the upper regions, came to Ephesus. And finding some disciples he said to them, "Did you receive the Holy Spirit when you believed?" So they said to him, "We have not so much as heard whether there is a Holy Spirit." And he said to them, "Into what then were you baptized?" So they said, "Into John's baptism." Then Paul said, "John indeed baptized with a baptism of repentance, saying to the people that they should believe on Him who would come after him, that is, on Christ Jesus." When they heard this, they were baptized in the name of the Lord Jesus. And when Paul had laid hands on them, the Holy Spirit came upon them, and they spoke with tongues and prophesied. Now the men were about twelve in all. (Acts 19:1-7)

4. THE TESTIMONY OF PAUL

Paul himself said, *"I thank my God I speak with tongues more than you all."* (1 Corinthians 14:18)

VOCAL GIFT THREE INTERPRETATION OF TONGUES

...to another the interpretation of tongues...
(1 Corinthians 12:10)

We briefly mentioned this spiritual gift in the section above. Now we will look at it in greater detail. The Greek word translated here as "interpretation" is *"harmeneia."* Its root meaning is "explanation." Here it is best understood as the "full interpretation" of a word spoken through tongues. Its specific use is the spiritual ability to give the meaning of words spoken in an unknown language (tongue). As mentioned above, this gift is always given to edify the church.

> *Otherwise, if you bless with the spirit, how will he who occupies the place of the uninformed say "Amen" at your giving of thanks, since he does not understand what you say?* (1 Corinthians 14:16)

The interpretation may be given by the one who speaks in tongues. If that person does not have this gift, someone else should interpret when the tongue is spoken in the church. Consider Paul's instruction to the church in 1 Corinthians 14:27, *"If anyone speaks in a tongue, let there be two or at the most three, each in turn, and let one interpret."* If an interpretation is not given this gift will not edify. It may actually bring confusion

215

rather than unity to the body of Christ. Consider the teaching in 1 Corinthians 14:33, *"For God is not the author of confusion but of peace, as in all the churches of the saints."* If your use of a spiritual gift is producing confusion rather than the Shalom of the Lord, you are not using the gift properly. This must not be allowed to happen in open church meetings.

As with all spiritual gifts, it is appropriate to pray for this particular verbal gift of the Spirit. Paul makes this very clear in 1 Corinthians 14:13, *"Therefore let him who speaks in a tongue pray that he may interpret."* Who does Paul say should speak with tongues? His answer is that every believer baptized in the Holy Spirit should possess and use this spiritual gift. Now add to that the instruction that all who speak with tongues should pray for the gift of interpretation. The conclusion is that we should seek and pray for both gifts.

EXAMPLES

Here are some things scripture teaches about the gift of interpretation of tongues:
1) This gift is necessary (1 Cor. 14:22)
2) The gift of interpretation of tongues is for the church (I Cor. 12)
3) This gift has been used all through the history of the church
4) This gift was never taken out of the church
5) Paul taught the church at Corinth to use this gift (I Cor. 14)

AS CHRISTIAN DISCIPLES WE SHOULD EXPECT THESE GIFTS

Do not be deceived, my beloved brethren. Every good gift and every perfect gift is from above, and comes down from the Father of lights, with whom there is no variation or shadow of turning. Of His

*own will He brought us forth by the word of truth,
that we might be a kind of firstfruits of His creatures.* (James 1:16-18)

God is a good and faithful Father who gives freely to us.
He always gives good and perfect gifts. His gifts come to bless
us and not to harm us. They are given to bless the work of the
church in proclaiming the Gospel of the Kingdom. He never
gives a stone when we ask for bread. I am always asking for
fresh bread from Heaven. The Lord Jesus came as the bread of
Heaven. He is the living Word of God. When I cry out for fresh
bread, I am seeking more of Him and more of his Word to build
up, strengthen and comfort the body of Christ. Remember what
He said about seeking the Holy Spirit. Believe it. Receive it and
begin to operate in all kinds of spiritual gifts.

*If you then, being evil, know how to give good
gifts to your children, how much more will your
heavenly Father give the Holy Spirit to those who
ask Him!* (Luke 11:13)

Remember, God desires to fully equip every disciple for
service. He wants to elevate you into the image of His creation.
He wants you to be more than you are right now. His desire is
for you to reach your full potential. He gives spiritual gifts to
equip you for the work of the ministry assigned to you. He is
not a stingy giver. All of the spiritual gifts are given to equip
the saints for God's purposes. Earnestly desire these gifts. Keep
pressing in for more. Remember that your first move in seeking
gifts is to pursue love. The more love you have the more He can
trust you with power and authority.

Again I remind you that as a disciple of Jesus Christ, you
should desire and seek these gifts. If you have not been desiring
gifts, you are not being obedient. This kind of behavior does
not honor the Lord. It does not bring Him glory. It does rob

Him of some of the joy He experiences when believers minister as He created them to serve. Think about what is being taught in James 4:2c-3, *"Yet you do not have because you do not ask. You ask and do not receive, because you ask amiss, that you may spend it on your pleasures."* God gives to those who earnestly seek. This is important for us to know. If you are not receiving all these things, you may need to find out if you are asking amiss. If you are not asking correctly, then you have a wonderful opportunity to repent and return to the fullness of your anointing.

In the body of the church, all of these "gifts of the Spirit" should be present. The absence of gifts should alert us to error in the church. When you recognize the absence of gifts, it should lead you to repent and return. Remember, gifts come after the baptism of the Holy Spirit. If you have not been baptized by the Holy Spirit ask the Lord to do this. You may also want to find a spirit filled believer to pray for you and lay hands on you to impart this gift.

Pray for Holy Spirit baptism that you might receive these spiritual gifts. Pray constantly for the gifts that you might produce the fruit of the Spirit. Pray that through these gifts you will demonstrate and prove that you are becoming who you are meant to be in Christ. It is unnatural for any believer to continue in the absence of these gifts. It is time to become natural. It is time for you to be gifted to move in the supernatural ministry of the gospel of the Kingdom. Amen?

PRAYER

For this reason I bow my knees to the Father of our Lord Jesus Christ, from whom the whole family in heaven and earth is named, that He would grant you, according to the riches of His glory, to be strengthened with might through His Spirit in the inner man, that Christ may dwell in your hearts through faith; that you, being rooted and grounded in love, may be able to comprehend with all the saints what is the width and length and depth and height—to know the love of Christ which passes knowledge; that you may be filled with all the fullness of God. Now to Him who is able to do exceedingly abundantly above all that we ask or think, according to the power that works in us, to Him be glory in the church by Christ Jesus to all generations, forever and ever. Amen. (Ephesians 3:14-21)

Summary

Seeing the Unseen Ream

How to See and Become Who You Are

The Lord spoke to me one morning and revealed that another falling away is beginning in the church now. I was given another vision in the training room of Heaven and saw several people walking side by side. When they reached a certain point they paused and then went separate ways. The separations seemed very peaceful, but my past experiences of the parting of ways between people has been anything but peaceful. It takes a great deal of emotional energy to cause two people who have gotten very close to suddenly part ways. I asked to understand how this could be so peaceful, and the Lord told me that the ones who remained were living in His Shalom Glory and they will experience peace no matter how tumultuous these situations may be. He was demonstrating in the vision how it will be in our experience when people decide to stop walking with us on our spiritual journey. Many of you have experienced the pain of separation as well. This word of the Lord for you today, is to stay in His Glory, and let Him saturate you with Shalom in spirit, soul, and body.

Then the Lord began to minister to those who were still walking with Him. The Spirit revealed that we are being told about this separation in advance so that when it comes we will not be surprised or experience any traumatic spiritual injuries. We know that this has to happen. We also know that it will not be a pleasant time. However it will be a time of increase in your gifts of the Spirit and in the level of your anointing. After each of these separations, I saw the Lord releasing more and more spiritual gifts. I saw Him placing His right hand on each person to release an increase of authority and anointing. My thoughts were directed by the Holy Spirit to 2 Thessalonians 2:1-3a, *"Now, brethren, concerning the coming of our Lord Jesus Christ and our gathering together to Him, we ask you, not to be soon shaken in mind or troubled, either by spirit or by word or by letter, as if from us, as though the day of Christ had come. Let no one deceive you by any means; for that Day will not come unless the falling away comes first,"*

It is very important at this time to exercise control over your thoughts and emotions. Remember 1 Corinthians 14:32-33, *"And the spirits of the prophets are subject to the prophets. For God is not the author of confusion but of peace, as in all the churches of the saints."* We must not get into fear or anxiety during this time. Remember that as Paul taught, God is the author of peace not confusion. In this season, we need to hold to His Word and meditate on the power statements which will keep us free from oppressive spirits. Meditate again on 2 Timothy 1:7, *"For God has not given us a spirit of fear, but of power and of love and of a sound mind."*

Always remember that the Lord calls you to stand strong in the face of the enemy. Do not fear! Do not be anxious! For the Lord your God is with you. Think on the question asked by Paul, *"If He is for you, who can be against you?"* Look again at Philippians 4:6-7, *"Be anxious for nothing, but in everything by prayer and supplication, with thanksgiving, let your requests be made known to God; and the peace of God, which surpasses all understanding, will guard your hearts and minds through Christ Jesus."*

May you be fully equipped in this hour to serve the Lord in strength and resilience! May you be filled with the peace which exceeds all your understanding! May your eyes remain fixed on Jesus! Follow Him closely at all times! He will never leave you nor forsake you! Trust in Him always and continue to accomplish His purposes in your life and ministry! Amen and Amen!

HOW WILL YOU BE KNOWN?

One of the presuppositions of this work is that everyone has the potential to become more of who they were created to be. Many people have no idea who they are in Christ Jesus. This knowledge is essential if you plan to complete your purpose and reach your destiny in the Kingdom of God. When you see, understand and become who God created you to be, you will experience fulfillment and joy in your service for Him. We began by examining a very powerful fact. The Lord has a plan for your life. One of the best expressions of this fact is found in the book of Jeremiah, "*'For I know the plans I have for you,' declares the LORD, 'plans to prosper you and not to harm you, plans to give you hope and a future. Then you will call upon me and come and pray to me, and I will listen to you. You will seek me and find me when you seek me with all your heart. I will be found by you,' declares the Lord,*" (Jeremiah 29:11-14a, NIV)

It is God's will for you to live out His plan for your life, but He will not force you to do it. He created you with free will and He always honors that part of who you are. It is His will that you be filled with hope as you become more and more aware of how awesome His plan is for you. There are at least two powerful ways that you and others can get an understanding of who you were created to be. You will be known by the fruit you bear in your life and work. If you are bearing good spiritual fruit, you can know you are following God's plan. The more fruit you see manifesting in your service, the more you will be assured that you are moving toward the goal of becoming all He created you to be. You will also give joy, honor and glory to Father God in the process.

> *"When you bear (produce) much fruit, My Father is honored and glorified, and you show and prove yourselves to be true followers of Mine."* (John 15:8, Amplified)

The second way you become known is through the spiritual gifts released to you by the Holy Spirit. As these spiritual gifts manifest in your work, you will be known by others through your gifting. Paul tells us there are nine gifts of the Spirit. In chapter twelve of the first letter to the Corinthian Church, Paul lists these nine specific and unique gifts of the Spirit. Each of these gifts has a purpose in the kingdom of God. It is important to remember that they are all given for the edification of the church.

> *Even so you, since you are zealous for spiritual gifts, let it be for the edification of the church that you seek to excel.* (1 Corinthians 14:12)

These nine spiritual gifts can be viewed as consisting of three groups of three. One set of three can be described as gifts of revelation. Revelation gift number one: "the word of wisdom." We see this at work in the ministry of Paul. He was told by the Holy Spirit to go to Rome (Acts 19:21), however he wasn't told when, why or how. The Spirit gave him a word of wisdom one night and told him why (Acts 23:11). As he stood before King Agrippa and Festus, the Holy Spirit gave Paul another word of wisdom and showed him how this would happen. He was also told when he was supposed to go (Acts 26:31). Later, the Spirit of God gave Paul another word of wisdom to prevent the death of all those on board the ship on the way to Rome (Acts 27:31-34).

The second gift of revelation is "the word of knowledge." While napping on the roof of a house, a message came to Peter from the Lord. He was told by the Holy Spirit that three men sent by the Lord were seeking him. When Peter was obedient to this word of knowledge, salvation began to spread into the Gentile world. It became clear that all people are equal in the eyes of the Lord. He is the creator of all people and His love is for the entire world. You can validate this through the words of Jesus spoken in John 3:16, *"For God so loved the world that He gave His only begotten Son, that whoever believes in Him should not perish but have everlasting life."* In Peter's ministry this awesome move of God began in the home of a Roman Centurion named Cornelius (Acts 10:9-17).

The third gift of revelation is "the discerning of spirits." With this gift you can discern both the workings of the Holy Spirit and the workings of demonic spirits. It is critically important to discern these things if you are going to minister effectively. This gift is given to protect you and the entire church. Through this gift the Lord helps you to understand and to know what is happening in the spiritual realm in order to increase your effectiveness in ministry.

When we minister in other nations, we are often confronted by shamanist spirits who seek to block the work of the Holy Spirit. The Holy Spirit quickly reveals these people to us so that we can deal with their witchcraft and block the curses they try to release. Paul had an experience like this. It is recorded in the book of Acts. As you read this passage in Acts, notice that Paul discerned the occult spirit before the man spoke.

> *But Elymas the sorcerer (for so his name is translated) withstood them, seeking to turn the proconsul away from the faith. Then Saul, who also is called Paul, filled with the Holy Spirit, looked intently at him and said, "O full of all deceit and all fraud, you son of the devil, you enemy of all*

*righteousness, will you not cease perverting the
straight ways of the Lord? And now, indeed, the
hand of the Lord is upon you, and you shall be
blind, not seeing the sun for a time."* (Acts 13:8-11)

The second set of three spiritual gifts can be described as "power gifts." These gifts are the spiritual gift of faith, gifts of healings, and the working of miracles. The power in the gifts is not the power of man, but the power of God. He has chosen to release this power through you as you partner with the Holy Spirit in ministry. All of these gifts work by the authority and power of God and at the same time demonstrate the spiritual power needed to help win the lost.

There are many examples of the gift of faith in the New Testament. One of my favorites is the account of the woman who touched the wings of Jesus' prayer shawl and was instantly healed of an issue of blood which had been going on for a long time. Jesus actually felt power flowing out from Him to her when this happened. He attributed her healing to her faith. She took an action step and released healing faith. Jesus said, *"Be of good cheer, daughter; your faith has made you well."* The gift of faith can release the same power in your ministry when you become who you are in Yeshua ha Messiach.

A great example of using the gifts of healings is seen among the seventy followers (see Luke 10:1) Jesus sent out two by two as ministers of the Kingdom. He told them to heal the sick and they followed His commands. When they returned, they were very excited about the outcome of their mission trip. The report of their work is recorded in Luke 10:17, *"Then the seventy returned with joy, saying, "Lord, even the demons are subject to us in Your name."* I like this account because it clearly demonstrates that these gifts were extended far beyond the original twelve disciples. They are also available to you and to me.

We often look at the ministry of Jesus to see the working of miracles. Yet the Bible gives us many examples of this being done by the disciples. Both Peter and Paul raised people from the dead. Another example is described in Acts, Chapter Three. Peter encountered a man with a birth defect. He had been disabled for his entire life because his body was not correctly formed in the womb. In an instant a creative miracle was released to finish his development. He was totally restored. He could walk and jump without going through any physical therapy. This is not normal. It is supernatural. Normally physical therapy is required to slowly develop the motor skills needed to move in this way.

The third set of three spiritual gifts can be described as verbal gifts because they all involve speech. These gifts are the spiritual gift of prophesy, the gift of different kinds of tongues, and the interpretation of tongues. As with the other gifts, these are not of natural origin. They are all supernatural manifestations of the gifts of God given by the Holy Spirit. All of these gifts are given to build up, encourage and comfort the body of Christ.

You can find a great example of all these three vocal gifts on the Day of Pentecost recorded in chapter two of the book of Acts. After being baptized with the Holy Spirit and fire, they received the power from on high promised by Jesus. The 120 followers rushed into the street and began speaking in tongues. The people present that day were given the gift of interpreting the tongues. Then Peter received a prophetic word which gave him an understanding of what they were experiencing. The Spirit let him know that this was the fulfillment of a prophecy given through the prophet Joel. The result was a huge harvest of souls for the Kingdom of God.

All of these spiritual gifts are available to you and me. If you are willing to receive them, they will be released as the Holy Spirit wills. As you receive and minister in these spiritual gifts you will grow more and more into the image of who you were created to be. Others will begin to know who you are by the gifts operating in your ministry. You will also understand more and more fully each day who you are in Christ as this gifting process continues.

Are you becoming all the Lord destined you to be? Are you producing fruit for the Kingdom of God? Are you demonstrating who you are as you manifest the gifts of the Holy Spirit? You should be growing daily in all these areas. When these things manifest in your life and ministry, it will bring glory and honor to our Lord. It will also give Him joy in the fulfillment of His ministry to you.

> *But we all, with unveiled face, beholding as in a mirror the glory of the Lord, are being transformed into the same image from glory to glory, just as by the Spirit of the Lord.* (2 Corinthians 3:18)

It is critically important for you to seek these gifts of the Spirit and to produce fruit fit for the Kingdom of God. This is how you accomplish God's plan for your life. This is how you reach your full potential. This is how you will become who you are in Christ Jesus. The Bible directs us to desire spiritual gifts. Remember what Paul wrote in 1 Corinthians 14:1, *"Pursue love, and desire spiritual gifts..."* It is un-natural for a believer to fail to produce fruit or fail to desire spiritual gifts. It is God's will for you to constantly pursue more love and to seek all the spiritual gifts.

PRAYER

> *And this I pray, that your love may abound still more and more in knowledge and all discernment, that you may approve the things that are excellent, that you may be sincere and without offense till the day of Christ, being filled with the fruits of righteousness which are by Jesus Christ, to the glory and praise of God.* (Philippians 1:9-11)

FINAL VISION REPORT

As you rest in the Lord on Shabbat, meditate on who you are in Christ! This morning the Lord was teaching again in the classroom of Heaven. He gave a series of visions to me of people walking around with their heads bent over as if ashamed of who they are. They were showing a kind of false humility which is not of the Lord. They appeared to be too shy and timid to stand up for the Lord. This false sense of shame had robbed them of the authority and power the Lord gave them when He commissioned them to do His kingdom work. Then I heard the Lord say, "This is not how you are to live! You must be bold in these days! You must stand strong in the gospel of the kingdom of God! Be strong and courageous! Do not live in fear! I am with you! What do you have to fear?"

How many times did the Lord say this to us? I counted over 328 instances where the Word of God tells us not to fear or be anxious. How many more times must He say it for us to live in it? As I was growing up in the church, the spirit of religion was in control and teachers were saying that timidity and a kind of false humility were the same thing as piety and righteousness. They taught that the only alternative to this lifestyle was a life of spiritual pride which goes before a fall. They were sincere in what they taught. It was all they knew, because the same things had been taught to them. They were sincere, but sincerely wrong. Thank God that we have been set free from these false teachings and from the spirit of religion. I believe the freedom this gave to me is one of the reasons why I hold so dearly the words of Paul in 2 Timothy 1:7, "*For God did not give us a spirit of timidity, but a spirit of power, of love and of self–discipline.*" Some translations substitute the word "fear" in this passage for the word "timidity." Timidity has its origin in fear, and that doesn't come from the Lord.

I started to meditate on who we are in Christ. Paul says that we are "*more than conquerors through Him.*" (Romans

8:37) Those who are in Christ have gone beyond judgment and condemnation: *"There is therefore now no condemnation to those who are in Christ Jesus, who do not walk according to the flesh, but according to the Spirit. For the law of the Spirit of life in Christ Jesus has made me free from the law of sin and death."* (Romans 8:1-2) There is no longer any enmity between God and those who are in Christ: *"Peace to you all who are in Christ Jesus. Amen."* (1 Peter 5:14b) One more thing: *"But of Him you are in Christ Jesus, who became for us wisdom from God—and righteousness and sanctification and redemption"* (1 Corinthians 1:30) Think on these things and reclaim all that the Lord gave to you when you were sealed in Christ Jesus! Amen!

My prayer for you today is the same prayer which Paul spoke over His spiritual son, Timothy. *"Hold fast the pattern of sound words which you have heard from me, in faith and love which are in Christ Jesus. That good thing which was committed to you, keep by the Holy Spirit who dwells in us."* (2 Timothy 1:13-14) I say it again, "Hold fast to that which has been given to you through the Holy Spirit!" Amen and Amen!

A FINAL REMINDER

You were taught, with regard to your former way of life, to put off your old self, which is being corrupted by its deceitful desires; to be made new in the attitude of your minds; and to put on the new self, created to be like God in true righteousness and holiness. (Ephesians 4:122-23, NIV)

Appendix One

13 ATTRIBUTES OF THE LORD

I have been intensely studying and reflecting on the attributes of the Lord since I first began to work on the book, "Seven Levels of Glory," published in June 2013. I have studied these passages in many different translations of the Bible as well as in the English version of the "Tanakh" (Jewish version of the Old Testament translated directly from the Hebrew). Each translation has its own strengths and weaknesses in clearly presenting the thirteen attributes of the Lord. I have chosen parts from several versions in working through the list below. This concept of the attributes of the Lord was likely first presented in The Chumash which is a very old and detailed study of the Torah in a variety of languages. You don't really need to be concerned about these various texts. I am simply giving some of the sources for this list of attributes.

> *And he (Moses) said, "Please, show me Your glory." Then He (Adonai) said, "I will make all My goodness pass before you, and I will proclaim the name of the LORD before you. I will be gracious to whom I will be gracious, and I will have compassion on whom I will have compassion."* (Exodus 33:18-19)

Now the Lord descended in the cloud and stood with him there, and proclaimed the name of the Lord. And the Lord passed before him and proclaimed, "The Lord, the Lord God, merciful and gracious, longsuffering, and abounding in goodness and truth, keeping mercy for thousands, forgiving iniquity and transgression and sin, by no means clearing the guilty, visiting the iniquity of the fathers upon the children and the children's children to the third and the fourth generation." (Exodus 34:5-7)

1. GOD OF MERCY BEFORE A PERSON SINS.

In some versions, both attributes one and two were expressed as the Lord declared His name to Moses as the Lord, the Lord God (Hebrew Adonai, Adonai Elohim). The name Adonai always carries a connotation of mercy. Here it is mercy given before a person sins.

2. GOD OF MERCY AFTER A PERSON SINS.

The name Elohim speaks of the God of Justice revealed in the second attribute, however it is not spoken alone. The Lord said, "Adonai, Elohim." This means that even in His attribute of justice He is still first and foremost merciful.

3. COMPASSIONATE

4. GRACIOUS

5. LONGSUFFERING (or slow to anger)

6. ABOUNDING IN GOODNESS (kindness to the thousandth generation)

7. ABOUNDING IN FAITHFULNESS (truth and faithful to fulfill His promises)

8. MAINTAINING LOVE TO THOUSANDS

9. FORGIVING WICKEDNESS/INIQUITY (intentional sin with premeditation)

10. FORGIVING TRANSGRESSIONS (intentional sins from a rebellious spirit)

11. FORGIVING SIN (unintentional sins or missing the mark)

12. DOES NOT LEAVE THE GUILTY UNPUNISHED

13. CAUSES THE NEGATIVE EFFECTS OF THE PARENT'S OFFENSES TO BE EXPERIENCED BY THEIR CHILDREN AND GRANDCHILDREN, EVEN TO THE THIRD AND FOURTH GENERATIONS

This last attribute also reflects the mercy of Adonai. Through these negative effects, future generations can be inspired to repent and return to the Lord so they can be restored.

Appendix Two

PRIEST AS HEALER

And you shall be to Me a kingdom of priests and a holy nation. (Exodus 19:6)

To him who loves us and has freed us from our sins by his blood, and has made us to be a kingdom and priests to serve his God and Father—to him be glory and power for ever and ever! Amen. (Revelation 1:5b-6, NIV)

And they sang a new song: "You are worthy to take the scroll and to open its seals, because you were slain, and with your blood you purchased men for God from every tribe and language and people and nation. You have made them to be a kingdom and priests to serve our God, and they will reign on the earth." (Revelation 5:9-10, NIV)

The three passages above present a very beautiful yet somewhat mysterious picture of who we were created to be and who we are in Jesus Christ. In conferences, I normally ask people to say aloud: "I am a priest." Then an interesting question emerges. What does a priest do? Leviticus was the Training Manual for priests in the time of Moses. Is it still appropriate for believers today? I believe it is also for today when you study and understanding it from a perspective this side of the cross. The entire sacrificial law was fulfilled in the death and resurrection of Jesus Christ. As a believer, you do not need to go back and learn all those rules and procedures. Jesus has already done it all for you.

There are some powerful lessons in the book of Leviticus which are important for kingdom priests today. One interesting aspect of the training is to understand that the role of a priest is to minister to the Lord (Leviticus 7:35) and bless the people (2 Chronicles 30:27). Most churches today do the opposite. They minister to people and then spend a little time blessing the Lord. Think about how the quality of our service to the Lord might change if we went back to doing it His way. I believe this is exactly what the Lord is calling us to do in this season. I believe the most important outcome will be to see our service to people as a method of releasing His blessing to His people. In order to do that, we need to spend much more time in the Holy Place ministering our praise and worship to Him. We need to come before Him daily as obedient priests working to do what we see Him doing and to say what we hear Him saying. This is ministry unto the Lord.

Most people who claim to be part of the kingdom of God and priests in His service don't study the manual. I think that one of the reasons for the reluctance of many to study the manual is that it just doesn't' make sense to them. It doesn't seem scientific. For example: to test the faithfulness of a wife the book says to put some dust from the floor in consecrated water and have her drink it. If she has been unfaithful, her stomach will swell. There is nothing in the dust or the water which would produce this effect. In essence, it is describing something supernatural.

I am not recommending the use of this test. What I am trying to say is that the work of a priest is supernatural. It is not based on human logic or scientific methodology. Yet it works because the Lord is in it. All we are doing is taking steps of faith which can activate the power of God to work miracles. Another example is the woman who touched the wing of Jesus' tallit and was healed. There was no magic in the fabric. It was the activation of her faith. Jesus confirmed this by saying that her faith made her well.

Many of the footnotes in English versions of the Bible focus intently on trying to identify diseases from the text of Leviticus and explaining how we should see them today based on recent medical knowledge. I believe they are totally missing the point. As a Kingdom priest, you don't heal with medicine. You heal with the power of God being released through gifts of healings. All of these are supernatural and you cannot explain them with examples from nature, science or medicine.

> *There He made a statute and an ordinance for them, and there He tested them, and said, "If you diligently heed the voice of the Lord your God and do what is right in His sight, give ear to His commandments and keep all His statutes, I will put none of the diseases on you which I have brought on the Egyptians. For I am the Lord who heals you."* (Exodus 15:25b-26)

As you study the manual for priests, always remember that the instructions in Leviticus are supernatural and intended to get your eyes focused on the Lord as your healer. It is the same in the New Testament. Think about the instructions in James 5:14, *"Is anyone among you sick? Let him call for the elders of the church, and let them pray over him, anointing him with oil in the name of the Lord.* Now picture this: someone comes to you with a sore toe. For them this is very serious and it affects their whole body. If you do what James recommends, you put olive oil on their head and lay hands on them to be healed. Olive oil on the head has no physical effect on their toe. Touching their head or shoulder has no effect on their toe, yet they get healed. Why? It is supernatural and it is based on faith as referenced in the next verse in James, "*And the prayer of faith will save the sick, and the Lord will raise him up. And if he has committed sins, he will be forgiven.*" Once again the healing comes by faith. It is supernatural.

God is still the healer. All He asks is for us to follow His supernatural healing remedies. This sounds simple enough until you consider that He also asks you to stay spiritually clean. How does that help to produce the healing? This too is supernatural. For the things of God to work in your life and ministry, you must be close to Him. He has standards for those who want to be close. Check it out in the passage below.

> *Who may ascend into the hill of the Lord? Or who may stand in His holy place? He who has clean hands and a pure heart, who has not lifted up his soul to an idol, nor sworn deceitfully.* (Psalm 24:3-4)

You can clean your hands in the natural, but how do you make them spiritually clean? How can you wash away the stain of sin or the misuse of touch? In the same way, you can refuse to get into idolatry. You can refrain from swearing deceitfully, but, how do you get a pure heart? What method can be used to make your heart pure after it has been stained? This too is supernatural. Think about it from the perspective of your priestly manual.

> *This shall be a statute forever for you: In the seventh month, on the tenth day of the month, you shall afflict your souls, and do no work at all, whether a native of your own country or a stranger who dwells among you. For on that day the priest shall make atonement for you, to cleanse you, that you may be clean from all your sins before the Lord.* (Leviticus 16:29-30)

None of the things done on Yom Kippur are natural pro-
cesses. The Lord supernaturally makes His people pure when
they obey. Should we continue to meet the Lord on Yom Kippur?
I believe we must. Check out what the Lord said in Leviticus
16:34, *"This shall be an everlasting statute for you, to make
atonement for the children of Israel, for all their sins, once a
year."* We have been grafted in to the root system of the children
of Israel, and we haven't outlived "everlasting" yet. Something
has changed for us. Jesus fulfilled it all.

Today, we meet with the Lord on Yom Kippur from this
side of the cross. Think about this: Yeshua was both of the
Yom Kippur sacrifices. He died to cover our sin and make us
spiritually pure. Barabbas was not the scapegoat, and he didn't
carry our sins away. Yeshua did that. When you accept Yeshua
as your savior, you are made pure. Not by what you have done,
but by what He did for you. The name Barabbas actually means
"Son of the Father." When the people cried out for Barabbas,
they were prophetically crying out for Yeshua the true Son of
the Father.

Instead of trying to do something which will result in our
cleansing on Yom Kippur, we come to the Lord's appointed time
to renew our covenant with Him through Yeshua ha Messiach.
In one sense we see that with Yeshua, every day is a type of
Yom Kippur. We don't have to wait for another year or a specific
day. We can repent and return to Him at any time, and He will
put His covering over all our past mistakes, failures and sins.
Hallelujah! Thank you Lord!

Are you a priest in the kingdom of God? If you have been
born again and Spirit filled, you need to see yourself this way
from now on. In fact, you are a much more special kind of priest.
You are a priest in the order of Melchizedek. As you read the
passages below reflect again on what Jesus said in John 14:12,
*"Most assuredly, I say to you, he who believes in Me, the works
that I do he will do also; and greater works than these he will do,
because I go to My Father."* You may need the seer anointing

to fully grasp all these powerful and wonderful truths. Pray for the Lord to open your spiritual eyes, spiritual ears and heart to perceive these things. Ask the Spirit of truth to guide you into all truth and help you to become all the Lord created you to be.

> *So also Christ did not glorify Himself to become High Priest, but it was He who said to Him: "You are My Son, Today I have begotten You." As He also says in another place: "You are a priest forever according to the order of Melchizedek";* (Hebrews 5:5-6)

> *And having been perfected, He became the author of eternal salvation to all who obey Him, called by God as High Priest "according to the order of Melchizedek,"* (Hebrews 5:9-10)

OTHER BOOKS BY
THIS AUTHOR

"A Warrior's Guide to the Seven Spirits of God"–Part 1: Basic Training, by James A. Durham, Copyright © James A. Durham, printed by Xulon Press, August 2011.

"A Warrior's Guide to the Seven Spirits of God"–Part 2: Advanced Individual Training, by James A. Durham, Copyright © James A. Durham, printed by Xulon Press, August 2011.

"Beyond the Ancient Door" – Free to Move About the Heavens, by James A. Durham, Copyright © James A. Durham, printed by Xulon Press, April 2012.

"Restoring Foundations for Intercessor Warriors" by James A. Durham, Copyright © James A. Durham, printed by Xulon Press, May 2012.

"Gatekeepers Arise!" by James A. Durham, Copyright © James A. Durham, printed by Xulon Press, February 2013

"Seven Levels of Glory" by James A. Durham, Copyright © James A. Durham, printed by Xulon Press, June 2013

"100 Days in Heaven" by James A. Durham, Copyright © James A. Durham, printed by Xulon Press, August 2013

"Keys to Open Heaven" by James A. Durham, Copyright ©
James A. Durham, printed by Xulon Press, November 2014

"Appointed Times" – The Signs and Seasons of Yeshua, by
James A. Durham, Copyright © James A. Durham, printed
by Xulon Press, December 2014

"A Fire Falls" – Moving into Holy Spirit Fire, by James A.
Durham, Copyright © James A. Durham, printed by Xulon
Press, February 2015

These Books plus teaching CDs and DVDs are available
online at:

www.highercallingministriesintl.com